Robert L. Preston

How to Prepare for the Coming CRASH

Published by

HAWKES PUBLICATIONS
156 W. 2170 S. (Box 15711)
Salt Lake City, Utah 84115
BOOKSTORES CALL:
1 - 800 - 453-4616
(Toll Free to Caller)

IN UTAH CALL:
—487-1695—

The material in this book has been gathered through the research facilities of the American Research Institute, P.O. Box 449, Provo, Utah 84601, of which the author is President.

ACKNOWLEDGEMENTS

The author is grateful to the writing of the following economists and financial consultants for the knowledge gleaned from their work and their perceptive insight into the economic practices of our nation: Paul Bakewell, Harry Browne, Henry Hazlitt, William F. Rickenbacker, Murray N. Rothbard, and Jermone F. Smith. Appreciation is also expressed to Linda Adams for her innumerable corrections of the manuscript, to J. Ben Skonnard for the hundred and one things he did to assist in the production of the book and the design of the cover. Last but certainly not least I wish to thank my wife Florene and our children for the long days and nights they sacrificed without a husband and father that this book might be produced.

The Author

*Dedicated to my parents
who were married in 1929
and know what a depression is.*

First Printing, November, 1971
Second Printing, January, 1972
Third Printing, February, 1972
Fourth Printing, March, 1972
(10,000 copies in print)

Fifth Printing, April, 1972
Sixth Printing, April 1972
Seventh Printing, April, 1972
Eighth Printing, June, 1972
Ninth Printing, November, 1972
Tenth Printing, December, 1972
Eleventh Printing, December, 1972
Twelfth Printing, February, 1973
Thirteenth Printing, March, 1973
Fourteenth Printing, April, 1973
Fifteenth Printing, May, 1973

(200,000 copies in print!)

Enlarged edition with keyed bibliography.

PREFACE TO THE 15th PRINTING

From our mail and many discussions with people from all walks of life across the nation, we have learned that even bankers, financial advisors and economics professors and many others who *ought to know,* simply do not understand the creation of money and the funding of the national debt. Therefore, as we go to press for the 15th time in less than two years, we have decided to slightly expand our explanation of the Federal Reserve, the influence of the banking industry on the Federal Reserve, the national debt and the creation of money. We hope that this enlarged explanation will help the American people to more significantly grasp what is happening to THEIR money!

We have also added a short postscript to the section "When It Will Happen" in an attempt to keep the book as current and relative to the date of its purchase as we can in this very fast-moving world in which we live.

Finally, I would like to say that the rapid acceptance of this book by the public goes to show that the American public is a great deal more aware and intelligent than they are generally given credit for. Once again it demonstrates what Thomas Jefferson said so long ago, that the best way to solve our problems is to "enlighten the people." I believe in America, and the American people! I believe that what the people of this great nation need is *more* truthful information and *less* government intervention.

The Author,
Provo, Utah
April; 1973

Table of Contents

Section One

Why It Will Happen

TODAY EVERY AMERICAN STANDS ON THE BRINK OF A PERSONAL DISASTER! HIS HOME, HIS INCOME, HIS FAMILY, EVEN HIS VERY LIFE ARE SERIOUSLY THREATENED.

THE COMING CRASH

A tremendous economic crash is about to destroy the entire financial structure of the United States. The end result will be a depression of a magnitude never before experienced in this nation. Millions of people will be out of work. Millions will starve. Riots, killings, and plunderings will sweep the nation. Disease will gnaw its way into the lives of millions more. Cities will become jungles infested with half-starved humans preying upon the weak, the sick, the old and the defenseless. Everywhere there will be the haunting hunger of the young and the innocent, looking up with hollow eyes, begging, pleading for just a morsel of food, a tiny morsel that is not there to give.

When will it come? It has already started. It started in 1913. It has come so far now that there is no turning it around. Those who are in control know that troubled times are ahead, they know that the situation is grave, but they are sure that they can control it just as they did in 1929. They believe that they can turn it to their advantage when the right time comes. But like a Frankenstein monster it will rise up and bring down the entire house around their own heads.

MONEY

But let us begin at the beginning. First, let us examine a subject we are all interested in. Money! Why are we interested in money? We cannot wear it, and we cannot eat it. We are interested in money because of what it can get for us. It can get for us the things we need and want, things that will make us happier than if we have to do without them.

THE BEGINNING OF MONEY

In the beginning of man's relationship with other men, he simply traded items he had that other men wanted for things he wanted. But as more people and more items became involved, trade and barter became more difficult and inconvenient. Gradually men settled on items, as a medium of exchange, that were universally needed. In the early days of society in Europe, cows, good for meat and milk and leather, were used as a medium of exchange. They were accepted because they had some value to nearly everyone; and though the individual who had just accepted them in trade might have had plenty of cows at the moment, he knew that someone would come along soon that would want the cows and would be willing to give him something that he wanted in exchange for them. Thus cows came to be used as money. In fact, our word "fee" comes from the German word for cattle, and our word "pecuniary" comes from the Latin word for cow.

REAL MONEY

However, cows were subject to the deteriorating value of all living matter, they were difficult to store, they were difficult to transport; in short, though valuable, they were inconvenient. As time passed, men became quite impressed with all of the things they were learning to do with metals. Some of these metals were very handsome and had some wonderful properties with which they could be worked.

14

They could be used for all sorts of needed and desirable items. One of the most useful was a yellow metal called gold. It had very good properties. It could be hammered into the thinnest and finest of sheets without breaking into pieces. It could also be drawn into the finest of wire. It could be melted easily and cast into ornate and intricate forms. It would also take a beautiful polish and could be made to shine like a mirror. And best of all, it did not tarnish. How desirable it was; but it was hard to find, it was not plentiful in the earth, and one had to give many cows to obtain this beautiful metal with which to make so many beautiful things. Another metal was much like it, but not quite so rare and not quite so fine; this, of course, was silver.

Because of their great usefulness, and their very limited supply, gold and silver soon became quite valuable. Since they were far more convenient and far more stable and just as desired as cows, they soon became used as money. For the sake of convenience, these metals were eventually cast into forms having a specific weight and value. Thus came into existence gold and silver coins--this was money. *It was valuable because it could be used to buy something its owner wanted, and it could always be converted into something of value and use itself--a ring, silverware, a gold watch--then it could be melted down and used again as money, having lost none of its value. This knowledge of the usefulness and thus the value of gold and silver made them the standard of exchange of the world.*

THE BEGINNING OF BANKS

Of course, to get it you had to give something of equal value--the back-breaking labor of digging it out of the ground or panning it out of a stream, or food, or clothes, or tools--something of value to those who had it. Those who were in the position of rule, of government, sought to

15

extract taxes from their subjects in order to acquire vast fortunes of this precious commodity of gold and silver.

Once wealth began to be accumulated in large amounts and large purchases were made, it became difficult to move all of the required gold and silver to complete the transaction. Soon merchants began to deal in the storage of and sale of gold and silver. They would issue a receipt for the amount of metal in storage. The owner could then trade his receipt for whatever he wanted, and the new owner of the receipt was thus the new owner of the precious metal. More and more frequently the new owner would leave his valuable metal with the merchant and likewise trade his receipt.

PAPER MONEY IS NOT WEALTH

Eventually the merchant of the metals devised a plan of giving receipts that were for only part of the wealth, but he would give enough of these receipts so that they totaled up to the amount that the customer had stored there. This allowed the customer to spend some of his wealth with a receipt worth so much and keep the rest of his receipts to use later for some other purchase. Thus the merchant of the precious metals became the banks, and the receipts for the metals on deposit became the paper representative of the valuable gold and silver he had on deposit.

It is important to realize that it was the gold and silver that was wealth. *The paper issued was only a receipt, only a representative of the wealth. The paper had no real value. You could not use it as you could the precious metals to make various items of value and of use which could always be converted back into the form of coins without loss should there ever be a need. Paper dollars have no intrinsic value; it is only what they represent that has any value.*

BANK LOANS

Finally the time came when the banker began to realize that there was never a call for more than about twenty percent of the real money he had on hand. If the banker had, say, deposits of $1,000 on hand, his clients would only withdraw, and others would put back in, less than twenty per cent. In other words, only $200 was actually being worked. "Why," thought the banker, "should I just let that other $800 lie there collecting dust? I'll loan it out to some of the merchants at a nice interest. They can give me the right to take some of their property and sell it if they can't pay up." Now, of course, this wasn't the banker's money; it was the depositors' money. But since they didn't know what the banker was doing, it didn't bother the depositors.

CREATING MONEY OUT OF NOTHING

After the banker had loaned out his depositors' $800, he found that the man that he loaned it to, and many of the people this man spent it with, put a large amount of it right back into the bank. "How wonderful," he thought. "I'll just set 20 per cent of this aside and loan out the rest of it again." In this manner, the bank had created money out of nothing. The money he was loaning was, on the largest part, merely bookkeeping entries. Since most of the money stayed in his bank, he was able to loan out the same money several times. Thus on the initial deposits of say $1,000 the banker eventually loaned and was paid back $4,000 or $5,000. Plus interest.

A RUN ON THE BANK

Now if no one became worried or suspicious, everything went along just fine. But suppose one day the banks were just a little short on ready cash when a big withdrawal was to be made, and they had to stall for time till they could rake up the money. The depositor becomes frightened that the bank doesn't really have his money and he wants it all, so the bank rakes it up and gives it to him. But he tells his friend that he thinks the bank is in trouble and his friend, too, goes and cashes in. Then others do the same. This is called a run on the bank; and of course, the bank can't come up with all the money; so it is forced to close.

DEPOSIT INSURANCE

During the twenties and thirties many banks were forced to close in just this manner. There are still banks being closed in the United States every day in just this manner. To prevent this from happening, the banks have joined together to form an insurance pool, each placing a certain percentage of its deposits in reserve in this master pool. They know that there may occasionally be a heavy drain on one bank or another and that they will be able to draw on this master pool held in reserve to solve the temporary crisis. This is one of the purposes of the Federal Reserve System and Federal Deposit Insurance Corporation. Of course, they rely on the law of averages; and as long as everything even goes halfway right they will be able to cover the emergency in this bank and that bank. But there is no way that they can guarantee all of the accounts in every bank at once. The F.D.I.C. has only $1.40 to insure each $100 of deposits. If everyone withdrew all his money on the same day, or even the same week, it would break every bank in the nation.

THE BEGINNINGS OF CENTRAL
OR GOVERNMENT BANKS

However, the most important development with the management of money came in the discovery that even governments and kings run short and have to borrow money to meet the needs of state once in a while. This had been discovered by several bankers throughout Europe in the 17th and 18th centuries. We shall just consider one of these. He was Mayer Amschel Bauer, an itinerant merchant in Germany in the late 1700's. Eventually he settled down and opened up a little shop in Frankfurt. Over the door he hung a sign on a red shield; as a result of the sign, he eventually came to be known as Rotschild, or Rothschild, meaning ''red shield,'' in German. The House of Rothschild sold and dealt in coins, rare and otherwise. A frequent visitor to the shop was the prince and many of his court. Because sometimes the prince was in power and sometimes he was not, he needed a place to keep his money when he had it and a place to borrow it when he didn't. Gradually Mr. Rothschild found himself in the national finance business.

THE POWER OF GOVERNMENT BANKERS

But Mr. Rothschild realized that if the king, who was all-powerful when he was in, should decide not to pay back the loan--or even if he were killed--well, that wouldn't be too good. Therefore, he hit upon a two-fold plan. The first thing was always to have money loaned to an opposing king that he could bring into play against anyone who might give him too much trouble. The second thing was to force the king, as part of the terms of the loan, to give him control over the money, the banking of the nation. Mr. Rothschild saw that it was the man that held the purse strings of the nation that really ruled. He once said, ''Give me control over a nation's currency and I care not who makes its laws.''

THE TAKE-OVER OF EUROPE AND ENGLAND

These national banks that Mr. Rothschild set up came to be known as Central Banks.[1]   Mr. Rothschild had five sons. One he kept in Germany with him, to take over when he passed on; the others he sent to the major cities of Italy, Austria, France and England. They had learned well from their father and soon were in charge of important banking and investing firms in each of their respective nations. Gradually, other great banking dynasties arose; but as each one came along, they took great care to co-operate with each other and keep the secrets of the business to themselves.

THE RISE OF AMERICAN FINANCIERS

Eventually it became obvious that the United States was going to become one of the richest and most powerful nations on earth, and these English and European bankers wanted to get in on the deal.[2]   In the United States there had developed several important and very successful banking and investment firms. Soon they began to have partners buy into their firms from Europe and England. Two of the most important of these firms were the Rockefeller and Morgan firms; another of the firms was called Kuhn, Loeb and Co. They were all located on Wall Street in New York, of course.

THE FINANCIAL CONSPIRACY

In Europe and England these international bankers had become part of a conspiratorial plan to unite the world into a central government and gain control of the wealth of the nations.[3]   They believed that once they had control of all of the wealth of the nations they could end all wars. They believed they could more evenly distribute the wealth among the people. They believed that by gaining control they could eventually get control of the nations politically. They planned to use their power and influence to help those who would teach in the schools, those who would preach in the churches, and those who would write in the presses the things that would help them unite the world under their government.

FINANCING COMMUNISM

When Karl Marx--and later, Lenin--came along, these wealthy bankers and businessmen put up the money to help them. Clinton Roosevelt and Horace Greeley put up most of the money to publish the communist "Manifesto."[4]   Later John Fels, an American soap manufacturer, gave a large sum to help Lenin when he was in London trying to get his revolutionary movement started.[5]   Still later, many other wealthy capitalists on Wall Street put up hundreds of millions of dollars to finance Lenin. It is known that Lenin paid back to the Kuhn-Loeb firm at least 600 million gold rubles.[6]   One of these men, Jacob Schiff, according to his grandson, bragged that he had personally put up $20 million.[7]   The man who had headed the project of getting money for the communist cause was a member of the Board of Governors of the Federal Reserve, Paul Warburg.[8]

THE CONSPIRATORIAL TIE

It was this same Paul Warburg that had been sent to the United States from the International Banking Fraternity in Europe and England to help the American bankers set up a system similar to the one which the Fraternity had in Europe allowing the bankers to gain control of the finances of the American government. [9]

SECRET ORIGIN OF THE FEDERAL RESERVE

Beginning in the year 1907 with a leave of absence from the Kuhn-Loeb firm at a salary of one-half million dollars per year, Paul Warburg went up and down the width and breadth of the nation teaching influential bankers of the country the advantages that would be theirs if they would just co-operate and set up a Central Bank for this country as bankers had done so well in Europe and England.[10]

By 1910, Warburg had convinced enough of the key bankers that, traveling incognito under assumed names, these bankers, representing all the important firms in Wall Street including Rockefeller and the Morgans, met in a secret meeting on Jekyll Island off the coast of Georgia.[11] It was later admitted by those who attended that meeting that it was there the groundwork was laid for the Federal Reserve Banking System. So secretive was this meeting that 18 years later Paul Warburg felt it was still best not to reveal what went on there; and to this day no outsider knows, except that it was then and there that the plan was agreed upon to set up the Federal Reserve.

PASSING THE FEDERAL RESERVE ACT

When they first tried to put the Federal Reserve Act through Congress, Senator Nelson Aldrich, under the control of the Rockefellers, was used as a sponsor; but that was easily seen through and the bill was quickly defeated. But because of Mr. John D. Rockefeller's financial contributions of up to $40 million at that time, the University of Chicago owed him a few favors.[12] Thus a couple of the associates of the University of Chicago were used to write up a new banking bill, and it was submitted by someone not so easily identifiable with Big Banking. In 1913, the Federal Reserve Act was passed.

SOME SAW PROBLEMS

But not everyone in Congress was blind to what this was going to mean to the nation. Henry Cabot Lodge, Sr., said, "The bill as it stands seems to me to open the way to a vast inflation of the currency....I do not like to think that any law can be passed which will make it possible to submerge the gold standard in a flood of irredeemable paper currency."[13] The father of the famous aviator, Charles A. Lindbergh, Sr., told the Congress, "This act establishes the most gigantic trust on earth....When the President signs this act the invisible government by the money power, proven to exist by the Money Trust investigation, will be legalized....The new law will create inflation whenever the trusts want inflation....From now on depressions will be scientifically created."

FEDERAL RESERVE GOVERNMENT OWNED

Theoretically, the government owns the Federal Reserve Banks.[14] The various banks which join the Federal Reserve System are required to put up a deposit with the system. This amounts to 16 percent for city banks, 12 percent for rural banks and even less on savings accounts.

On this deposit they receive 6 percent interest, which in the banking game is like losing your shirt when compared to what you could get if you had it back in your bank where you could loan it out four or five times. But this deposit forms the master pool that we mentioned earlier and is there to prevent any one or two banks from running dry if a sudden run should occur on them.

This money does not provide these banks with any stock in the Federal Reserve. However, there are 12 banks spread strategically over the United States where these pools of reserve funds are maintained; and. they do own a special kind of stock in the system. However, this is nonvoting stock and could be retired by the government at will. It cannot be sold nor borrowed against. In reality the word "stock" is a misnomer. The act requires that each of these twelve banks put up 6 percent of their capital as security and receive 6 percent per year on that amount. This interest payment in 1963 amounted to $24 million. The share of capital stock put up by the United States Treasury at the outset has also been earning 6 percent interest, and between the years 1947 and 1969 the government earned $7 billion interest on its investment in the Federal Reserve System.

FEDERAL RESERVE NEVER AUDITED

Although the Federal Reserve controls all of the currency--just look at the face of your dollar bills, and you will see they are all *Federal Reserve Notes* (a note is an I.O.U.) --and controls virtually all of the credit rates of the nation's banks, they have never been audited by the Government Accounting Office (GAO). Over the years various congressmen have attempted to have this done, but they have never succeeded. For a great many years Wright Patman, Chairman of the House Banking Committee, has tried numerous times to get the Congress to force a government audit of the Federal Reserve. Each time, the Congress has refused to go along. It is a rather appalling thought to realize that a special group has been created which is so powerful that Congress is afraid to force it into an audit. (Perhaps too many important people would be embarrassed.)

FEDERAL RESERVE PRIVATELY CONTROLLED

While the Federal Reserve was ostensibly created for the purpose of protecting the public's interest in the nation's money supply, it has, in reality, become the exclusive tool of the bankers. Although the President is allowed to appoint one member to the seven-man Board of Governors every two years, and these men must be ratified by the Senate, their appointments for fourteen-year terms are virtually never questioned; and all have been men favorable to the banking industry--almost all being bankers themselves. In fact, the first man ever selected to this board was none other than Paul Warburg (the international banker who was the chief architect and instigator!) who had immigrated here from Germany for that very purpose. Keep in mind that he held that position during the greater period of time that we were engaged in World War I with Germany, where his brother Max was the head of the Bank of Germany.

In addition to the banker-and-financier control of the board itself is the broader and more powerful control of the "Open Market Committee" --the main policy-and-decision-making body of the Federal Reserve. The following information is quoted from a government document prepared by the House Committee on Banking and Currency, and will demonstrate the control of the private bankers over the Federal Reserve System:

It is indisputable that the commercial-banking community wields considerable power within the Federal Reserve....Further, the central decision-making body, which decides whether the System will press the ac-celerator or the brake, *is the Federal Open Market Committee....Here, then, is the private banker influence.* [15]

A further demonstration of the independent power of the Federal Reserve is a statement given in a Joint Economic Committee of the U.S. Congress in August of 1962, by Mariner Eccles, Chairman of the Federal Reserve Board. While Congressman Wright Patman asked, ''Is it not a fact that the Federal Reserve System has more power than either the Congress or the President?'' Eccles under oath then responded, ''In the field of money and credit, yes.''[16] Here is the open testimony of the head of the Federal Reserve that this privately operated banking system is not only in-dependent of the President and Congress, but is actually *superior to them* in the control of the nation's money supply. Does it not seem incredible that an organization, which was created by the Congress, has amassed so much power that it now considers itself more powerful than its creator? Nevertheless, this is the case! If you need further proof that the Federal Reserve is in reality a privately operated banking system rather than a government agency, simply write them and ask for some information, then look at the envelope from the Federal Reserve when it comes. If it is a government agency, it will have its postage paid free with a government frank. If it is a private agency it will pay postage like everyone else. I can tell you right now, they pay the postage--because they are NOT a government agency!

As further evidence of the superior power of the Federal Reserve over the officers of the government, I cite the fact that in 1969 the Federal Reserve raised their interest rate, causing the economy to shrink the following year by *$20 billion.* When Secretary of the Treasury David Kennedy was asked by *U.S. News and World Report* if he approved of the Federal Reserve's doing such a thing, he responded, "It is not my job to approve or disapprove. It is the action of the Federal Reserve."[17] Thus, from behind the scenes, the Federal Reserve System is manipulated by private, unseen owners. When profits are made--and they are enormous-- they are divided up among the owners of a select group of banks that participate in the system. This may be as illegal as robbing a bank, but they have been doing it for more than 50 years. No one has been able to stop them.

MANUFACTURERS OF INFLATION

Through this great control the bankers manipulate the money supply in such a way that they reap billions of dollars a year in tax-free profits. As you may have observed, the government occasionally spends more money than it takes in. In order to cover its expenses, the government is forced to borrow the funds it lacks in income, to pay its bills. Each week the Secretary of the Treasury authorizes the issuance of Treasury bills, notes or bonds. These government securities are placed for sale with the Federal Reserve, which has the option to buy them or sell them through their Open Market operation in New York.

When the Federal Reserve decides to buy the government securities, it simply creates the funds *out of nothing* by writing a check on its own bank to make payment; *or,* it has the Department of Printing and Engraving print up sufficient currency to cover the cost. Whenever the Federal Reserve orders currency from the Department of Printing and Engraving, its only cost is the cost of the paper, ink and labor. On the average, the Federal Reserve pays only $1.50 for each $1,000 in face value which it receives. The great tragedy is that when the Treasury Department and the Federal Reserve swap pieces of paper, this becomes part of the National Debt and you and I pay interest in the transaction. Some of this eventually winds up going back into the Treasury as income; but a great deal of it fattens the holdings of the Federal Reserve. It must be kept in mind that this money is literally *created out of nothing* by the Federal Reserve and has no backing by anything; it is as worthless as if it had been printed in a gangster's basement! *THIS IS INFLATION.*

However, the greatest amount of profit is created for the private bankers by the operation of the Open Market of the Federal Reserve. Here Government Securities, which the Federal Reserve decides not to buy, are sold on the so-called "open market." Actually there is nothing *"open"* about it. There are a total of 21 banking and financing firms that are "licensed" to buy in this "open market." Although these 21 firms bid on these securities, they are not truly competitive, since they have many interlocking stockholders often disguised by elaborate *holding* companies. Through a clever manipulation of Federal Reserve banking procedures, these firms are able to create *out of nothing* the funds with which to buy these securities. This is achieved by using the government security as collateral, upon which a note is issued for one-fifth the amount; and the Federal Reserve loans the firm the money by depositing a credit for that amount into their reserve account. Based upon these cash reserves (which have been created out of nothing) the firm is now able-- *out of nothing*--to create the money (up to *five times* the amount in their reserve account) with which to buy the government note. This is how the national debt is funded--by allowing the banking industry to create money out of nothing and loan it to the taxpayer at huge profits.

$45,000-A-MINUTE PROFIT ON
THE NATIONAL DEBT

During the first 140 years of our nation's existence the government went into debt *less* than 2 billion dollars. During the 60 years since the Federal Reserve and the banking industry have been able to fund this debt out of funds they create out of nothing, the government has gone into debt more than 440 billion dollars! The profits on this debt (the interest that is paid on it each year) amount to the third-largest item in the Federal Budget. The interest alone now amounts to more than the entire cost of running the Federal Government when Franklin D. Roosevelt came into office. This interest payment is now costing the taxpayer *more than 45,000 dollars a minute.* The U.S. Government is in debt to the banking industry more than all the rest of the nations of the world put together. In 1971 the interest payment was so great--more than 21 billion--that the government had to borrow an additional $25 billion that year in order to pay the interest. Out of this money more than $18 billion went directly into the pockets of the wealthy stockholders of the banks which hold these government securities. Oh yes, keep in mind that this money is *tax-free.* In case you missed the significance of all this, keep in mind that a billion dollars, printed in one dollar bills, laid end-to-end, would reach all the way to the moon, a quarter-of-a-million miles away; and do it five times! A billion dollars spent at the rate of one thousand dollars a day would last for 2,738 years, and we as taxpayers pay more than 18 billion dollars a year to the private stockholders of the big banks that loan the government money which they create out of nothing.

SKYROCKETING INFLATION

The placing of unbacked money into circulation, either by currency or by check--for both are money--is *inflation*. Rising wages and prices are not inflation. They are merely the efforts of the business and working man to keep up with the loss of value of the inflated money. Inflation is the process of inflating the paper representatives of wealth without a corresponding increase in that wealth. For several centuries the world has found that a money supply based upon reserves in gold is the most practical. We have continued to inflate our money supply in ratio to our gold reserves to the point that, for all practical purposes, there is not a single ounce of gold backing it. Today the United States has a completely fiat money system. As this money is spent into circulation, some of it will wind up in banks as deposits for savings. Through the workings of the Federal Reserve Act each of these dollars has the potential of becoming part of the bank's loan base. This is a reserve fund that is set aside and from which *five* additional dollars in loan funds can be created *by the bank* for each dollar in the reserve fund. When we say *"created,"* we mean exactly that. The bank will use pen and paper to write checks to *create* the funds which it loans out. Since years of experience by the banking industry has demonstrated that most of this newly created loan money will *not* leave the bank, the remaining money will be loaned out again and again. Thus each dollar *created out of nothing* by the Federal Reserve, that finds its way into the bank's loan funds, multiplies itself no less than *five more times* and most likely eight or ten. Therefore, each inflated dollar that goes into circulation becomes the source from which many other inflated dollars spring. This results in further deterioration of the strength of the dollar and a continual loss in its purchasing power, further rises in wages and prices, more and more demands for devaluation, and the ever-looming spectre of a monstrous depression!

THE CAUSE OF THE CRASH

When you have a rubber balloon, it has just so much material in it, just so much rubber. Now that rubber has a certain amount of give, of stretch. When you begin to inflate it, it gives, but the walls get thinner and thinner. If you keep inflating it, eventually it will become so over-inflated it will break. The same thing is true of the economy. It has a lot of stretch and give, and it will take a lot of inflation; but the walls keep getting thinner, and just at the point where it is the biggest and most beautiful thing you ever saw, it will break.

Now if we kept adding more rubber to our balloon, we could keep on making it get bigger and bigger without harm, because we were adding to it that which gave it its value. If we could keep adding gold to the treasury, we could keep putting more dollars into circulation without harm.

THE CRASH IS IMMINENT

When we have only four cents' worth of gold backing each dollar, it is obvious that the inflationary balloon is not going to stretch much farther. *The crash and the depression that follows may occur at any moment from now on.*

MANY PEOPLE CAN SEE IT COMING

While every effort has been made to deceive the public, and quite amazing to me is the calibre of people who have been deceived, not everyone has had the wool pulled over his eyes. Back in 1959, people began to sense that something was going wrong with the finances of our money system. They felt insecure. They couldn't explain it.

Certainly they couldn't defend their fears before the host of super intellects in the economics departments of Washington and the universities. But in their own quiet way they began to do the only sensible thing they could have done. They began to store silver coins. The government said it was foolish--why they had lots and lots of silver. Just listen to what President Johnson had to say:

> *Some have asked whether silver coins will disappear. The answer is very definitely—No. Our present coins won't disappear and they won't even become rarities....If anybody has any idea of hoarding silver coins, let me say this. The treasury has a lot of silver on hand, and it can be, and it will be used to keep the price of silver in line with its value in our present silver coin. There will be no profit in holding them out of circulation for the value of their silver content.* [18]

EMPTY POLITICAL PROMISES

All of the bold and positive statements of the politicians to the contrary, the intrinsic good sense of most people has told them that this nation was in trouble and headed down the wrong road. Less than two years after President Johnson made his statement on silver coins, most of the true silver coins had been replaced by worthless nickel-plated copper ones by the government. How many are so naive as to believe that dollars with four cents' worth of gold, and dimes and quarters worth about two or three copper pennies are going to be able to maintain a nation's economy for very long.

ROBBING THE POOR TO PAY THE RICH

All of the laws in the world, making gold and silver illegal as money, will not alter the basic law of economics that says a man must receive value for value. When billions and billions of dollars created out of nothing first hit the market, they seem to stimulate it and make the economy expand; but actually in a short while they do just exactly the opposite. When nothing has been produced with that paper dollar, no service or product created of equal value to the amount shown, then instead of adding to or creating something within the economy, it robs it, draining away that amount of goods and services from the people and giving it to the ones that created it. The further down the line the dollar goes after it gets into the economy the less it does, and pretty soon it gets to be a negative factor. By the time it gets to the widowed, the sick, the poor, and the pensioned, it has become a big deficit that robs them, robs them of what they need so desperately. *Inflated paper money robs the needy and pays the money baron who created the monstrosity.*

TOO LATE TO TURN BACK

Once a government starts on this false money business, it has no choice but to ride it to the end. We are down the road too far to turn back. I began my study of this matter in the hope of finding a way to turn the tide. But the process is too far gone. Now what the government is trying and has been trying to do is to halt the inflation, or at least to slow its advance. But when they try to slow it down, the day of reckoning starts to catch up, business starts to slide, businesses fail, people get put out of a job, the unemployment rate climbs, the government gets frightened so it pumps more money into the economy.

TRYING TO CONTROL INFLATION

Here is how it works. Businesses want to expand and grow. That is good for the country; everybody is working and eating. To expand they need money, so they borrow the money from a lending institution. Some of that money, as we have seen, these institutions create from money they have on hand from their depositors. But in an expanding economy like the politicians want that is not enough, so the financial institutions borrow the money from the Federal Reserve.

The Federal Reserve controls the amount of money it is putting into the economy by the amount of its discount rate. When the rate is raised, that means that the banks cannot afford to borrow as much as before, and the amount of "new" money going into the market is reduced. If they really want to reduce the amount of phony paper money in circulation, they raise their interest rate quite high. This means that the banks down the line have to demand that the customer pay up his loan now or the bank will have to foreclose. The local banks are forced to do this so they can pay the money the F.R. is demanding from them. Conversely, when they want to fill the pipe line with more funny money, they simply lower the prime interest rate so that the local banks can borrow larger amounts and loan them out profitably. By finding out what the F.R. is doing with the discount interest rate, you can tell if they are trying to prop up or cool down the economy. This is what the government must try to do--control the inflation--they can't eliminate it; all they can do is try to control it.

RUNAWAY INFLATION

If the inflation is not held back, then the economy goes berserk. The paper dollars drop in value faster; wages and

34

prices rise and rise faster and faster, finally just skyrocketing; the government printing presses are going twenty-four hours a day trying to keep up; the prices are changing hourly. And finally it is hopeless, and the money is completely worthless; no one will take it. Then all the factories and stores shut down. Rioting, robbing, looting and all types of crime begin to stalk the streets. The cities turn into concrete canyons, with savages hunting down their prey of other human beings who might have food and drink. Blood flows like rain water in the gutters. It has happened before, in France and in Germany. Only this time, it will be worse than ever before. It will be worse because there are large segments of the population which have been brought up without morals. They will have no compunction in imitating the worst scenes from the most vile and savage books they have read and movies they have seen. They will torture without mercy and kill without reservation to get the things they are after. This will be the terror that is coming if we have runaway inflation. Because this was becoming a very distinct possibility, wages and prices were frozen. But this did not solve the problem. All it does is delay the inevitable result. The inevitable result will be a depression, a complete collapse of the economy. Price controls may head off runaway inflation, but it cannot hold up a depression.

THE COMING DEPRESSION

There is no question of whether we are going to have a depression. The only real question is When? But before we get into that let's examine what a depression is. A depression is a total loss of confidence in the economy of the nation. The snapping up of silver coins, even at prices far above their face value, is an indication that there is a serious loss of confidence in the nation's economy. The fact that people have lost so much faith in the value of the dollar that they keep wanting more of them for the same product or service is an indication of the serious loss of confidence in the nation's economy. Every step the government takes to adjust the nation's economy adds to the fears and suspicions of the people. At this moment the fears of the people that the country is about to go bankrupt are justifiably high and rising by the hour.

A NATURAL DECLINE

When people begin to fear that the economy is going to go broke, they tighten up on their spending. If the government would leave things alone, this would be healthy. Unemployment would go up, it is true. That is not good; but as we shall see, it could be a lot worse. As a result in the decline in spending and employment, prices would start to come down. This is not a result of a failing economy; this is simply the ''air'', the inflation, leaving the economy. But politicians fear declining prices and refuse to leave well enough alone.

PUMPING UP THE ECONOMY

More paper money is dumped into the commercial market through loans to the banks from the F.R. This excess money hits the economy with a bang and there is an immediate pickup in employment, pay raises and spending. This looks good at first glance. But this is all artificial; there is nothing real about it; it is phony. There has been nothing of value placed into the economy. The economy cannot grow unless something of value, in the way of goods and services, has made a contribution to the nation. A printed piece of paper does not add value to the nation; and when that piece of paper is able to purchase something that is of value for someone who produced it with practically no cost, it drains the economy of that much value.

For example, as stated earlier, it costs the F.R. approximately $1.50 to print $1,000's worth of bills. That $1.50 is the total contribution then of that $1,000. When the $1,000 is placed into circulation, it removes $998.50 more from the economy than it contributes. Now the first person to receive the $1,000 will pass it on to the next guy, and he will get part of the $1.50 value that is in that $1,000. After awhile, this $1,000 will have passed through several hands, each getting a piece of that $1.50. Soon the $1.50's worth of value will have been absorbed; and as the $1,000 is passed on, each person that receives it makes a contribution to make up the $998.50 deficit in the value of the bill. The further down the line the funny money goes the larger the amount of the deficit made up by the next person to receive it. That is why the non-producers, the sick, the aged, the pensioned, the widowed and the orphaned are hit the hardest.

So the people who can tell that they are making up a deficit in the money they receive start raising their prices for their goods and services to make up for the deficit, and we have inflation again.

DRAINING THE ECONOMY

When the prices start to rise too high and too fast, the money men don't want it to get out of hand so they attempt to remove some of the deficit by raising the interest rates to the banks and withdrawing some of the deficit money. With less money to loan that means the banks will be more selective. There will be more turndowns for loans, and businesses that were going to expand will have to curtail their plans. Job opportunities will not develop. Some people will be laid off. Spending will drop off, and that will cause another rise in unemployment. People will become frightened and start hanging onto their money again, and the economy will start to sink. But before it goes too far, the money boys plan to pump a little more funny money back into the economy; but, as we have seen, this will only make matters worse. Eventually, the ''experts'' realize that this vicious cycle is getting harder and harder to handle, and it is going to require more drastic measures.

THE PRICE FREEZE

In order to artificially pump up the economy without everyone raising his prices, the government decides to freeze and then regulate prices. Once this is done, they can artificially stimulate the economy with more funny money. This, at first, sounds like a good solution. But there is a very good reason why this will not work. Two groups of people begin to lose faith in the deception. The first group is the other nations of the world that have good sound currency that is backed by gold to a high degree. The second group is within the nation and they become concerned when the other nations become concerned.

THE OTHER NATIONS

Why should a nation that has worked hard not to spend more than it produces--a nation that has currency of real value--why should they accept a currency that has no real value? There is no reason after it reaches a certain point. As you know, many of the nations of the world have reached that point. They will give you less of their dollars for your American dollars today than they would have a year ago, or six months ago. So as the economy is inflated continually, even with the freeze, the real value of the dollar continues to shrink; and the other nations continue to demand more and more of our money for their money. In other words, they do the same thing the people over here did when the inflation kept coming--they keep raising their price. Eventually they will refuse our money altogether, it will be so worthless. The law may say you and I have to accept it here at home, but we can't make Germany, or France, or Switzerland take our dollars. Today, the American dollar is backed by four cents' worth of gold, but the Swiss franc is backed by 82 cents' worth of gold. Why should they exchange 82 cents' worth of gold for four cents' worth? There is no reason to and so they don't.

THE DEVALUATION

After price controls and continued inflation, the only thing the government can do is devalue the dollar. That means that they will voluntarily alter the exchange rate; that is, they will give more American dollars for foreign goods and services. How much more? That is a tough one. The government is walking a tightrope. They have to devalue enough to keep the rest of the nations from refusing our money, but they can't drop it so low that they will cause a panic at home. Most likely, the government will make secret promises to the other nations to devalue the dollar in stages so as not to trigger a panic at home. Conceivably, such a promise to install price controls was made in secret meetings with other nations six months or more before they were actually instituted here at home. This was probably done as an inducement to get the other nations to keep accepting our money. Probably the minimum amount of devaluation that will be acceptable to the other nations will be a 50 percent devaluation. The U.S. may try to get by with two 25 percent devaluations. But within the next few years the other nations would require that we devalue at least a total of 75 percent.

DEVALUATION AND YOU

At first it won't mean much to you. Then you will go to buy a Swiss watch, some French perfume or a German car. The price you will find after the 50 percent devaluation is exactly twice what it was before. That's right; it will cost you twice as many American dollars to buy in many foreign markets. Not all. Many Western economies are tied to ours, and they would have to devalue with us. Eventually many American prices would have to go up too; the price controls would have to allow all those who have to buy raw materials and parts for their products at these new high prices in foreign markets to pass the increase along to you. *What devaluation means to you is high cost of living.*

CONCERN AT HOME

This is the other group of people that become concerned with price freezes, continuing inflation, and devaluation. There is in any situation always a group of people who are astute observers of the passing scene. They know when something is going wrong, and they act accordingly. When this group begins to realize what is happening to the economy, and that it is going to crash in a complete collapse, they begin to liquidate their assets. They sell; they do not buy. Like the squirrel that senses a hard winter, they start storing up reserves for the hard times that lie ahead. These people will probably profit from the crash. They are certain to if they store up the right kind of nuts. This kind of conservative economics is wise, prudent and profitable, for the individual and for the economy. But there is another group that spells danger to the economy.

PANIC

The most dangerous element in the nation's economy is the nonprofessional speculative investor. These people have a little extra money so they dabble in investments here and there. They make up a sizeable total amount of investment stock. These people are always afraid something will happen to their investment because they feel they can't afford to lose it. They are nervous and jittery about the economy. They have been buying stocks on the market not because of their knowledge or faith in the company's ability to produce dividends, but they have been buying stock on the basis of what they thought it was going to do on the stock market. Today there is a great deal of this kind of investing in our economy. Every little negative occurrence tends to cause these people to dump their stock, making the market go down. This group reacts psychologically and anything could set them off. The worse the economy becomes, the larger this group becomes, and the deeper the psychological reaction becomes. This group is dangerous. It is this group that can upset the best-laid plans of the government and all of its controls. It is only a matter of time until this group will panic. Suddenly there will be a massive dumping of stock on the market and there will be no end. The situation is ripe and ready to happen; all it will take is some national occurrence of a negative nature to set off a panic wave, and the Great Depression will be here.

THE PLANNED PANIC

In addition to the accidental panic, there is strong evidence that a panic can and has been deliberately instigated. You will recall that Congressman Charles Lindbergh, Sr., had objected to the F.R. Act on the grounds that through it depressions could be created. Congressional investigations of the Crash in 1929 have indicated that it was deliberately manufactured. U.S. Congressman Louis McFadden, Chairman of the House Banking and Currency Committee, commented: "It was not accidental. It was a carefully contrived occurence...The international bankers sought to bring about a condition of despair here so they could emerge the rulers of us all."[19] What did Congressman McFadden mean, "emerge the rulers of us all"? There are two ways that this occurred, or at least partially occurred.

First, the international bankers had removed their money from the stock market long before the Crash and had placed it in investments in gold and silver. When a depression occurs, the individual with good money in his pocket is even richer than he was before, because now he can buy anything he wants for a small amount of money from people who have to sell because they are in desperate conditions. In this way, the international bankers are able to gain control of a great many businesses and corporations after the crash. The crash, then, is to the advantage of the rich with proper cash. A crash is to the disadvantage of the poor and those who have their wealth tied up in non-spendables. The cost of liquidating assets after the crash would be disastrous. Also the individual in debt with an income that will be seriously impaired during a depression is in serious trouble. The international bankers took advantage of these people; they foreclosed on mortgages and bought up assets for pennies on the dollar. Thus, when America emerged from the Depression, there were new owners of nearly every major industry--the international bankers.

The second way the international bankers "emerged as rulers over us" was that with the stress of the Depression, they were able to push a lot of emergency legislation through the legislature that socialized America. This is to the advantage of the bankers, because it increases the cost of government and requires deficit spending, which raises the national debt and increases the annual interest payment by the government to them. This means that you and I must dig up more money for taxes, to pay the interest to the international bankers. Thus, depressions are to the advantage of the international bankers, who have ready cash at their disposal to take advantage of the situation when the rest of us are destitute and desperate.

EXPERT TESTIMONY ON THE CAUSE OF THE '29 CRASH

Historian Ferdinand Lundberg states:

> *Various governmental investigating bodies have heard copious confessions to "Mistakes" and "errors of judgment" from the executive representatives of the multi-millionaire dynasties. But there were really no mistakes or errors of judgment. Except for the culminating debacle of 1929-33 everything happened according to plan, was premeditated, arranged, sought for.* [20]

One of the nation's foremost experts on economic depression, Murray Rothbard states:

> *Central banking works like a cozy compulsory bank cartel to expand the bank's liabilities; and the banks are*

43

now able to expand on a larger base of cash in the form of central bank notes as well as gold. So now we see, at last, that the business cycle is brought about, not by any mysterious failings of the free market economy, but quite the opposite; by systematic intervention by government in the market process. Government intervention brings about bank expansion and inflation and when the inflation comes to an end, the subsequent depression-adjustment comes into play. [21]

William Bryan, writing in *The United States Unresolved Monetary and Political Problems*, states:

When everything was ready, the New York financiers started calling 24 hour broker call loans. This meant that the stock brokers and the customers had to dump their stock on the market in order to pay the loans. This naturally collapsed the stock market and brought a banking collapse all over the country because the banks not owned by the oligarchy were heavily involved in broker call loans at this time, and bank runs soon exhausted their coin and currency and they had to close. The Federal Reserve System would not come to their aid although they were instructed under the law to maintain an elastic currency. [22]

HOW IT IS DONE

A crash can be instigated at almost any time by the will and direction of just a few people acting in concert together. It is hard for most people to realize, but it is nevertheless true, that the Rockefeller, the Kuhn-Loeb, and Morgan groups hold enough stock in enough companies and have enough control of the Federal Reserve Bank, that they could wreck the entire economy of the nation in just a matter of

44

days.[23] David Rockefeller, who heads the Chase-Manhattan Bank, has bragged that he is the most powerful banker in the world.

If the Federal Reserve were to raise its discount rate to banks, these banks would be forced to recall some of their loans and the economy would immediately begin to shrink. This would create a negative psychological climate. Add to this the dumping on the market each day before the stock market closed a significant amount of stock to depress the market and you would have in a few days a very serious trend. Each day the market would be closing down. Within a matter of days a panic would be precipitated, and there would be a run on the banks and a total crash of the stock market; and then it would be all over. A depression would be here. As insurance, the other Central Banks in England and in Europe might also raise their discount rates when the Federal Reserve does, thus forcing a withdrawal of foreign capital in the stock market and guaranteeing an almost immediate loan to stock brokers, which requires that a loan given to a stock broker must be repaid within 24 hours if called for by the bank. In 1929 this occurred on October 28, and the market crashed on the following day, October 29.

IT CAN HAPPEN AGAIN

Many people have tried to reassure themselves, in the face of mounting evidence to the contrary, that it could never happen again. They cite the great government controls that have been instituted. The last President described the American economy as being "absolutely sound," and the current President has declared that "poverty will soon be a thing of the past." Many economic experts have declared that the economy is now "depression-proof." "The Federal Reserve has a host of powers with which to regulate the economy. They can guarantee a steady stream of credit to stimulate the economy." "The many government programs--farm, highway, small business, public works--and the regulatory powers over the stock market, labor, industry and banks stabilize the economy." "Production of every major industry is at an all-time high. More people are at work and more people have more money than ever before." "The amount of gold leaving the treasury is insignificant, especially in view of the real strength of the nation which is our productive capacity, our gross national product."

Sounds reassuring, doesn't it? Until you realize that these are not comments made today. All of these statements were taken from the news stories in the papers of 1929, just before the Crash.[24] *It can happen again! In fact, the only real question is not if, but when?*

Section Two

What Will Happen

WHAT WILL HAPPEN

Because price controls have been installed by the government, we can eliminate the possibility of runaway inflation. That is, we can eliminate the symptoms of runaway inflation. There will be no galloping wage and price rise. The price controls will make sure of this.

What we will see is devaluation of the American dollar on the world market. This will push prices up a little more, but we will be able to live with that. But it will probably trigger a few recessions. That is, people will become cautious and fearful at the thought of the American dollar's being devalued and start holding back on their purchases. But once again the government will try to solve that with a little more paper money.

However, sooner or later the American people are going to lose so much faith in the dollar that many of them will refuse to accept it, and everyone will want to unload. The panic will start and overnight the market will crash and the little game of deception will be all over with. Of course there is always the possibility that the crash will be engineered. No matter how it comes about, deliberately or accidentally, the only thing that can really occur in the economy--the end result of everything--is going to be a crash.

THE BACKFIRE

As we have already seen, there is much evidence that the last depression was planned and to a large degree controlled. This time there will be no control. The coming depression is not going to be just a depression. It is going to be a complete and total anarchy.

Today there are thousands of people, young and old

alike, who have been alienated against our society, many for no real reason and many for very good reasons. This makes up a large--a very large--group of hundreds of thousands of people. Now, in the days of our fat, our wealth and our plenty, they are calling for the complete destruction of our nation. They want to blow it up and burn it down; and while there are many who might be inclined to agree and to follow, they will not, because they are having things too easy to make their angers hot enough to put forth the effort that it takes to destroy a great nation. However, you can be sure that when there are no jobs and there is no food, they will become very angry, angry at a system they are at the mercy of, but which they do not understand and cannot control. It is logical and understandable. It will be only natural that these people will want to destroy what they think is their enemy.

SHOPLIFTING TO LOOTING

During the past decade the rate of shoplifting has shot up at an appalling rate. In the college bookstores, from Stanford in California, to Yale and Harvard in the East, all have experienced the same thing. Shoplifting at campus stores is jumping 80 to 100 percent per year. Why? Because this generation has been taught that there is a new morality which does not have absolute rules. There are millions of young people, who have been carefully indoctrinated to believe that if they are sincere in their heart and believe they are working for a true and noble goal, then certain ordinary standards might be justifiably violated in order to reach their worthy goal.

This is not the fault of the young; they were taught by the adults. But not only the young steal from stores and employers; the whole moral structure has been carefully softened over the years, and theft from stores and employers by adults who should know better have multiplied by many hundreds of percent in the past decade. What will this mean during a depression? If people will steal when times are good, when "they never had it so good," what will they do when they "never had it so bad?" What will happen is wholesale looting.

BREAKDOWN OF MAJOR CITIES

The major metropolitan areas will become totally without law and order. Gangs, roving bands, bound by a common need and feeling of vengeance on society which has dealt them this cruel blow, will focus the first assault on the external vestments of society--the stores which hold within them the necessities of life, necessities they are now to be deprived of, not through some fault of their own, but because something went wrong with what they believe was a bad society anyway. They will overpower checkout clerks and take what they want. They will break windows and loot what they want. They will be joined and followed by timid, ordinary and average people that think, "Well, everybody else is doing it; and if I don't get mine this way, I won't get anything at all." The looting will be everywhere at once; and as the days pass by and more and more average people join in the fray, the police will be utterly helpless. The National Guard will be mobilized, of course. But they cannot hope to quell every riot and every looting all over the nation.

GUERRILLA WARFARE

The truly violent enemy will see this as the perfect opportunity to destroy society as they have come to know and hate it. The long-laid plans by these minority militant groups will be encouraged by the sudden breakdown of law and order and the failure of civic officials and employees to halt it. Their ranks of followers will begin to swell. Strengthened by these things, they will begin their all-out attack.

Every major city will be hit. Water, sewer, power, gas and communication lines will be blown up. There will be no radio--the transmitters and towers will be blown up--and no television for the same reasons. The cities will begin to be infernos of terror as bombs explode, gas lines erupt and spew uncontrolled fire everywhere. Doctors and other medical aid will soon become unavailable. Hospitals will become inundated and overburdened to the point of complete collapse. Vital drugs will be unavailable. Those with marginal health will not be able to stand the strain and will die. Cities will burn in uncontrolled fire, and the drafts created by the heat will create fire storms forcing the fire to whip across the cities at several miles per hour. The weak, the old, the sick, the very young, the defenseless will be assaulted for whatever they might have that would be desirable to their enemy. Unfortunately there are many people of the calibre of Richard Speck in this world. Only the restraints of society keep them in check. With a total breakdown of law and order, the Charles Mansons will come creeping out of the ground to kill, to maim, to torture and destroy for their sheer pleasure of bringing death and misery to other people. These are terrible thoughts to the average person, but they must be faced, for they are a reality.

In preparation for the writing of his book, *In Cold Blood,* the author Truman Capote spent several years with the men who had killed a Kansas Farm couple and their children. It was his testimony to the Congress that these men were killers and would kill again if they just had the opportunity. We may argue about the psychological causes and the possibilities of rehabilitation and correction all we want to; but when there is no law and order to protect us, multitudes of these people will manifest themselves. They do exist; and the recent wave of violent movies showing the most realistic scenes of blood and gore and cruelty and the wanton waste of human life will create the most macabre scene of viciousness ever seen on the face of this earth.

MARTIAL LAW

Long before things become as terrible as we have previously outlined, the governors and the President will have declared martial law. Anyone found disobeying the orders of the military or the police will be shot on sight. This will not solve the problem; it will only aggravate it. There will be a mobilization of the armed forces in an attempt to quell the disturbances across the land. But an army can only mobilize when it has a nation behind it with which to mobilize. It is one thing to defend a country and fight an enemy, and it is quite another to fight your own country. The AWOL rate will be enormous as most men will want to be home defending their own families. Officers who try to stop deserters would soon be shot. Bridges will be blown, highways destroyed, fuel supplies blown, rail lines and equipment sabotaged. No food will be available for the armies. In addition to this, there are many nations who would love to come up and take possession of this nation; and, seeing us in such a distraught position, will seek to take advantage of us. Invasions will be launched into our borders, and the military still available will have to be mobilized by the government, largely for national defense. It will not be as simple a matter to maintain law and order in this nation as most people think. If the depression is deliberately instigated, the instigators will find that the United States of the 1970's is an entirely different place from the one of the 1930's.

DISEASE

Without proper sanitary conditions in the cities-- sewage and water lines contaminated or destroyed--without medication and health care, with refuse piling up everywhere and dead bodies uncared for, there will soon be epidemics of disease sweeping through every metropolitan area. First will be simple dysentery, and following shortly on the heels of this will be such items as cholera, ptomaine, jaundice, typhoid, and bubonic plague. Millions will become violently ill; and millions will die without proper aid and care.

NO FOOD

The modern city is in reality a deathtrap. The food supply in all of the stores and warehouses combined cannot feed the city for more than a week. The food industry in America is in reality a modern miracle. Every day, by truck, by rail, by boat and plane come thousands of tons of food to the cities all across our land. If this supply should be interrupted for even a few hours, hardships on the food supply will develop. Anyone who can remember the food crises that developed during the ''Cuban Crisis'' in all of the major cities as panicky people swept the shelves of markets clean can imagine what it will be like during a real emergency. Food supplies will of necessity be confiscated by the military to feed the men that will have to defend the nation. As commerce and trade and transportation are deliberately interrupted by the guerrillas, the cities will be without food in a matter of days. Mass starvation will threaten the lives of millions of people caught without food supplies and with no means to get any.

THE REALITY OF IT ALL

I have not enjoyed writing the preceding lines. The thought of what this will all mean to the children fills my heart with such anguish that I cannot write of them. But this will be, to borrow a line from James Baldwin, "The Fire Next Time." When the depression comes--and it is coming--these things are what will happen. We can choose to ignore them, or disbelieve them, but it will not dissolve reality. *And just as surely as death comes eventually to us all, both small and great, so will the inevitable destruction, cruelty and horror of the next depression. It cannot be prevented--only prepared for!*

Section Three

When It Will Happen

WHEN IT WILL HAPPEN

The question everyone wants answered, of course, is When is this going to happen? It is doubtful that anyone knows the day or the hour. But there are several who know the general time period in which it will occur.

TRIGGERING THE DEPRESSION

As we have already mentioned, there are two approaches to the coming depression--the planned or the accidental. I am one of those in the minority who believe that it will be planned, and I have made some allusions to the fact that a secret conspiracy has existed for a long period of time in which the international bankers have attempted to gain control of the world, to run it as they think it ought to be run. They believe that once they are incomplete charge, they can do a much better job than anyone else can. This is not the time and place to detail the conspiracy. I have done so in complete detail, giving names, dates and places from its inception right down to its present members and activities, in a book entitled *Wake-Up America.*

If we take the conspiratorial view, we know that they want to take over the United States before the two hundredth anniversary of the founding of their secret organization, on May 1, 1776. As we have previously mentioned, they have provided the financial support for communism from its inception. Communism has been their tool to take over the world. A captured communist document during the Korean War revealed a twenty-year plan for the take over of the United States.[25] According to this document, this plan would reach its climax in 1973.

ANY NEGATIVE NEWS WILL DO

However, let's completely disregard the conspiratorial aspect. Let's assume that all of the manipulation of our currency and the development of inflation, price controls and the coming devaluation have been due to mismanagement. This means that the depression will come whenever those in charge of the economics of this country miscalculate just enough to start a panic. Actually, it could be almost anything. The death or assassination of the President could set off a Wall Street panic. It could be a resolution adopted by the United Nations pronouncing the United States guilty of war crimes and genocide in the Vietnam War. It could be the refusal of Germany to accept any more American dollars. It could be almost anything.

DEPRESSION PSYCHOLOGY IS HERE

Panic has already started. It started in the 1960's with the storing of silver coins. The germ of panic psychology is growing daily. The ratio of real money to paper currency is rapidly spreading. In 1966 it was 13 to 1; by 1968 it was 23 to 1. Although it is difficult to obtain up-to-the-minute statistics, a good estimate would be that by the spring of 1972, the ratio could be 28 or 30 to 1. Price controls have added to the psychology of panic already within the minds of many people. Devaluation, which is sure to come shortly, will add even more to this psychology of panic.

WATCH OUT FOR 1973

It could and is very likely to happen at any moment from this point on. After my study of the opinions of several economic experts, it is my "out-on-the-limb" prediction that it will occur before 1975. And as early as 1973. I pick 1973, because I believe that because of the political aspects of the election in 1972, nothing will be done by the money boys to upset the apple cart if they can possibly help it before the elections. This means that after the Inauguration in January of 1973, it will be necessary to devalue the American dollar at least 50 to 75 percent; and this could touch off the panic. President Nixon will not want to devalue the dollar before the elections. After the elections, whether he wins or loses won't make any difference. If he loses, he won't care because the next President will have to handle it. If he wins, he won't care because he can't be re-elected for a third term anyway. It is my belief that secret agreements have already been made by the United States with the international bankers, that after the '72 elections the American dollar will be devalued at least 50 percent. I believe that coupled with the built-up psychological fears of the American people, this will touch off a panic. *The panic is likely to occur as early as 1973.*

A KEY SIGN

Many people keep their eye on the stock market as the barometer of the depression. This is like locking the door after the horse is out. It's true the stock market will tell you *after* the depression is here. What you need to know is when the depression is almost here, *before* it comes, so that you can take care of those last-minute preparations. As we have already stated, it could happen at any time without warning- the machinery is in motion and the fuse has been lit.

However, there are two things to watch for in particular. The first is the prime interest and discount rate of the Federal Reserve Banks. If it is going up, get ready, because the economic screws are being tightened; and this could precipitate a crash at any time. Watch the prime interest and discount rate; if it is below 5 percent, then the economy should not fall into a depression unless there is a very bad news shock to the nation, such as the President's death. But if the rate starts to go up, watch out; it could happen any time. And the higher it goes, the sooner it will happen. The second sign is devaluation. This will be harder to pick up before it happens; but when it does happen, get ready; because a crash might occur at any moment thereafter.

STRAWS IN THE WINDS

Another telltale sign is the remarks of the President and the key members of the Administration. If they are not saying much about the economy, then it is a good sign things are not too bad at the moment, from the standpoint of official plans and pressures. But if they are talking about the economics of the nation a lot, then that means they have a lot of plans and pressures regarding the economy. The more they talk in a positive and reassuring tone--the more they deny any trouble--the more they deny any strong courses of action--the more you can count on the fact that they are about to do something serious. The more they deny devaluation is in process, the more you can be sure that it is.

For example, in England, the Chancellor of the Exchequer, Sir Stafford Cripps, denied categorically that the English pound would be devalued, making such statements as, ''complete nonsense;'' ''under no circumstances,'' and ''completely unfounded reports.'' The last such statement was on Sept. 6, 1949, and on Sept. 18, 1949, the pound was devalued. Cripps dismissed his deception by stating that, ''No responsible minister would possibly have done otherwise....''[26] When President Nixon kept assuring the people that he did not want price controls, that he didn't want Congress to even give him the power to have them, that he would never use them if they did, what did he do? He used them and froze wages and prices.

You can trust the people in government and economics to cover their intended actions with denials. And the louder and more frequent the denials are, the more sure you can be that that very action is imminent.

TIMING

You can almost always be sure that any major economic action taken by the government or the Federal Reserve Bank will be done on the weekend. Be especially attentive of weekend economic news and try not to leave yourself vulnerable economically over a weekend. It might turn out to be the "lost weekend."

POSTSCRIPT — APRIL, 1973

Many of the things which we had warned would occur *have occurred*. The devaluation has occurred right on schedule. However, the amount was not sufficient to solve the problems. More serious international monetary problems are ahead. No long-lasting solution can be created until there is control of U.S. inflation, and our imbalance of trade payments is satisfied. Since there seems to be no prospect of such a thing occurring, there will be periodic disturbances on the international monetary scene--float or no float.

Rising interest rates have occurred as we predicted. Currently, the discount rate is at 6 percent. However, inflation is continuing at a rapid clip, with wages and prices rising at a faster rate than at any time in the past 25 years.

Hesitation on the part of the Administration and the Federal Reserve to cool things off will result in sharp action to curtail the problem before the end of '73, most likely in September. Such actions will plunge the economy into a recession that will rapidly grow into a full-blown depression. The months ahead are fraught with serious economic danger to the American people--everything is moving just about as we have anticipated.

With the tightening of credit by raising interest rates and reserve requirements, the funds which have previously been available for business expansion are disappearing. Surplus funds for stock investing are disappearing. Mutual funds are sinking fast. Life insurance companies are rapidly dropping out of stock market investments. Small investors are leaving the market in droves. Bank investments are rapidly being curtailed in favor of loans at more attractive rates--an event which always coincides with and stimulates a decline in the market. Shortages are running at an all-time high, which result in higher costs and business failures. Confidence in the scandal-ridden Administration is sinking, and the general public is beginning to become very, very uneasy about the economy. Rapidly rising prices of gold and silver indicate world-wide fears over the entire international monetary situation as more and more of the big "in-the-know" investors move from *paper* to *solid* assets. All of this adds up to an ominous picture that spells *depression.*

Many people assume that when an economic "crash" occurs, it happens all at once. This is not so. What happened in October of '29 was only the beginning, and if that was all that occurred we would not be talking about it today. There was a sudden drop all right, but the long descent to the bottom after that lasted for three long years, not hitting the lowest point until '32. In our opinion the current "crash" began on January 12, 1973, with the raising of the discount rate to 5 percent and the subsequent drop in the stock market of 85 points in the next four weeks. The market will, we believe, continue to roller coaster downhill until the fall of '73, when it will take a sharp downturn due to efforts at that time to control inflation. As we said in '71, ''watch out for '73!''

Section Four

How To Prepare For It

HOW TO PREPARE FOR IT

The great depression cannot be stopped. There has never been a nation in the history of the world that has issued bogus currency and gotten away with it. In John T. Flynn's book entitled, *Men of Wealth*, the account is given of the reign of Louis XIV of France.[27] It seems the good King had spent the nation into bankruptcy. But along came the hero of the hour, John Law, with the perfect solution. Simply have the government gain control of all the standard wealth of the nation, that is, all of the silver and gold, and make it illegal to own it. The King did this, just as F.D.R. did with gold in our day. Then since the standard of wealth is now out of reach, simply substitute a new standard, one which the king, or government, can produce as much of as they want, like paper currency. So good King Louie did as Law instructed and put Mr. Law in charge of the Royal Bank. It worked like magic, for awhile. Then people became suspicious of the King's paper money and...well that is the end of the story, because at that point the whole thing came down on the King's head; and John Law, once hailed as the genius of the ''new economics'', who would do away with old-fashioned, outdated symbols of wealth like gold and silver, died in abject poverty. The system we have today is not new, and like all of those that have gone on before and were identical to it, it too is subject to the same end result.

It is said that those who will not learn from history are destined to repeat it. If this is true, then we are about to enter into a serious depression at any time. It has gone too far to stop, so the only thing to do now is prepare for it.

As we have previously mentioned, not everyone suffers in a depression; some even prosper. While ex-millionaires were committing suicide over a few dollars, others were becoming millionaires with a few dollars. The key is not how much you have, but where you have it!

TIME TO PREPARE

The time to prepare is now. Panics are psychological mavericks, and in mass psychology they are even more unpredictable. All of the necessary precursors are there. It may come at any moment, so the time to be ready is now. The suggestions that follow are good suggestions and will bring you through any depression as well as could be hoped for, but they do call for some drastic action that some people may hope to forestall till the last minute. This is, of course, everyone's prerogative. However, when a panic occurs, it occurs overnight. Within hours many of the alternatives that lay open to you before have been closed off. The time to act is now! This may cost you a little bit of profit here and there, but to delay one day too long may cost you nearly everything. In the city, the difference could be your life! *It is far better to be ready years too soon than to be one day too late.* The time to prepare is now!

YOUR VERY BEST INVESTMENT

The preservation and protection of your life and those of your loved ones is your very best investment. A portfolio of the finest blue chip stocks and bonds and bales of paper money will be as meaningful as dust in the wind when the depression hits. The first, the very first, item of importance will be food. It will not only serve to sustain you and your family, but it will be the best money you can have in many instances. I have a friend whose uncle bought a brand new car during the last depression. He paid 500 lbs. of potatoes for it.

COUNT ON YOURSELF

Don't depend on the fact that the Red Cross or some other emergency relief is going to come to your aid at this time. They probably will try to help in the beginning, but the magnitude of disaster will be so great that all of their supplies will be exhausted in just a few days. *The best person to count on is yourself.* Once you are prepared by following the suggestions in this manual, you will be prepared not only for the depression, but also for power failures, food and services strikes, long-term unemployment and illness, floods, earthquakes, tornadoes, hurricanes and war. It's the best insurance money can buy!

STEP NUMBER ONE

Just as a great building is built brick by brick and nail by nail, so you should prepare your program of self-preservation. The first thing to do is supply your vital needs. Next to air to breathe, your body needs water. So the first thing you do is make sure you have enough good drinking water stored for each member of your family for a period of two weeks. You can live quite awhile without food, but not without water. Secure your water supply first. One gallon of water per person per day is a survival amount. This is the most vital and inexpensive part of the program. Do this first; do it now!

STEP NUMBER TWO

Next to water is the regulation of body chemistry by medication for those who need it. If you are a heart patient, a diabetic, or have any kind of illness or condition requiring constant medication, your life will be in serious jeopardy without it. Go to your doctor and tell him you would like an extra prescription as a reserve to have on hand in case a strike or civil disturbance should temporarily cut off your regular supply. Always rotate medical supplies. Once your current supply of medication runs out, get your next regular refill but don't use it. Use that to replace the one you have in emergency storage and use it instead. This way you will always have fresh medication available. Build your medicinal reserve to cover at least a year's period if you can, but by all means do set aside a two-week's supply to start with.

STEP NUMBER THREE

Set aside a food stockpile for at least a two-week duration. The following information is taken directly from the U.S. Department of Agriculture's *Home and Garden Bulletin* No. 77 and is entitled, ''Family Food Stockpile for Survival.'' This is a nutritionally sound program for a two-week survival period and very well could be the most important investment you will ever make.

FAMILY FOOD STOCKPILE FOR SURVIVAL

FOOD

Every family should either build up and keep a 2-week supply of regular food in the home at all times or assemble and maintain a special 2-week stockpile of survival foods in the fallout shelter or home.

Survival foods may vary from a single cracker-type food, such as rye or wheat wafers or specially prepared biscuits, to a fairly complete assortment of familiar foods.

Stockpile foods should be in cans, jars, or sealed paper or plastic containers. Select foods that will last for months without refrigeration and can be eaten with little or no cooking.

Take into consideration the needs and preferences of family members, storage space, and ability to rotate the stored foods in family meals. Familiar foods are likely to be more acceptable in times of stress.

Kinds of food familiar to the family and suitable to store for emergency use are shown in table 1. Amounts suggested will supply the calories needed by one adult for 2 weeks. If your family consists of four adults, store four times the amount suggested in table 1. Teen-

TABLE 1.—*Guide for Reserve Food Supply*

Kind of food	Amount per person for—		Remarks
	1 day	2 weeks	
1. Milk	Equivalent of 2 glasses (fluid).	Equivalent of 7 quarts (fluid).	Each of the following is the equivalent of 1 quart of fluid milk: Evaporated milk: three 6-ounce cans; one 14½-ounce can. Nonfat dry milk or whole dry milk: 3 to 3⅔ ounces.
2. Canned meat, poultry, fish, cooked dry beans, and peas.	2 servings	28 servings (8 to 9 pounds).	Amounts suggested for one serving of each food are as follows: Canned meat, poultry: 2 to 3 ounces. Canned fish: 2 to 3 ounces. Canned mixtures of meat, poultry, or fish with vegetables, rice, macaroni, spaghetti, noodles, or cooked dry beans: 8 ounces. Condensed soups containing meat, poultry, fish, or dry beans or dry peas: one-half of a 10½-ounce can.
3. Fruits and vegetables	3 to 4 servings	42 to 56 servings (about 21 pounds, canned).	Amounts suggested for one serving of each food are as follows: Canned juices: 4 to 6 ounces, single strength. Canned fruit and vegetables: 4 ounces. Dried fruit: 1½ ounces.

4. Cereals and baked goods.	3 to 4 servings.	42 to 56 servings (5 to 7 pounds).	Amounts suggested for one serving of each food are as follows (selection depends on extent of cooking possible): Cereal: Ready-to-eat puffed: ½ ounce. Ready-to-eat flaked: ¾ ounce. Other ready-to-eat cereal: 1 ounce. Uncooked (quick-cooking): 1 ounce. Crackers: 1 ounce. Cookies: 1 ounce. Canned bread, steamed puddings, and cake: 1 to 2 ounces. Flour mixes: 1 ounce. Flour: 1 ounce. Macaroni, spaghetti, noodles: Dry: ¾ ounce. Cooked, canned: 6 ounces.
5. Spreads for bread and crackers.	According to family practices		Examples: Cheese spreads. Peanut and other nut butters. Jam, jelly, marmalade, preserves. Sirup, honey. Apple and other fruit butters. Relish, catsup, mustard.
6. Fats and vegetable oil		Up to 1 pound or 1 pint.	Amount depends on extent of cooking possible. Kinds that do not require refrigeration.
7. Sugars, sweets, and nuts		1 to 2 pounds	Sugar, hard candy, gum, nuts, instant puddings.
8. Miscellaneous	According to family practices and extent of cooking possible.		Examples: Coffee, tea, cocoa (instant). Dry cream product (instant). Bouillon products. Flavored beverage powders. Salt and pepper. Flavoring extracts, vinegar. Soda, baking powder.

agers are likely to need more than the amount in the table; younger children need less.

By including, each day, foods from the eight groups listed, members of your family can have a reasonably nutritious diet.

If necessary, include special kinds of milk and strained, chopped, or other specially prepared foods required for infants, toddlers, elderly persons, and others on limited diets.

Whenever possible, choose cans and jars in sizes that will fill your family's needs for only one meal. This is especially desirable for meat, poultry, fish, vegetables, evaporated milk, and other foods that deteriorate rapidly after a container is opened.

If your home food freezer is located in your basement or where you would have safe access to it after attack, you might count foods in it as some of your reserve supply.

Food spoilage in a well-filled, well-insulated home freezer does not begin until several days after power goes off. Food in large freezers will keep longer than food in small freezers. Once the freezer has been opened, foods should be used as promptly as possible.

Sample Meal Plans

Sample meal plans are presented on pages 74 and 75. These plans suggest the kinds of meals you could serve from the foods shown in the table on pages 70 and 71.

Half of the meals fit a situation where there are no cooking facilities. The other meals require facilities for heating water or food but not for any extended cooking.

The foods suggested are all fully cooked and safe for eating "as is" without cooking. (Home-canned meats and vegetables may be eaten without cooking if you are sure the canning equipment was in good working order and recommended methods of canning were used.) If you have provided a sufficient variety of canned foods in your reserve supply, it is possible to have reasonably well-balanced meals. However, because of limited space and in order to use fewer dishes, it may be more practical to serve fewer foods at a meal and make the servings more generous.

Storing and Replacing Foods

If you have prepared a fallout shelter, keep your reserve food supply there. If you have no shelter, keep it in that part of your basement where you will be safest in case of attack.

In homes without basements and in apartments, your food stockpile would probably be stored in the kitchen or in a storage closet.

To maintain the eating quality of your reserve food supply, keep

canned foods in a dry place, where the temperature is fairly cool—preferably not above 70° F. and not below freezing.

Protect food in paper boxes from rodents and insects by storing boxes in tightly closed cans or other metal containers; leave the foods in their original boxes. Keeping these foods in metal containers also extends the length of time they can be stored.

Eating quality was the first consideration in setting the maximum replacement periods given on this page. Many food items will be acceptable for a much longer period if storage temperatures do not usually exceed 70° F. Most of the foods suggested in table 1 would be safe to use after longer storage periods.

As time approaches for the replacement of particular food items, it is a good idea to use the food in family meals. As food items are used, replace them in the stockpile with fresh supplies. When you put in fresh supplies, put them at the back of the stockpile; keep older supplies in front.

Here are suggested maximum replacement periods for the kinds of food listed in table 1:

	Months
Milk:	
Evaporated	6
Nonfat dry or whole dry milk, in metal container	6
Canned meat, poultry, fish:	
Meat, poultry	18
Fish	12
Mixtures of meat, vegetables, cereal products	18
Condensed meat-and-vegetable soups	8
Fruits and vegetables:	
Berries and sour cherries, canned	6
Citrus fruit juices, canned	6
Other fruits and fruit juices, canned	18
Dried fruit, in metal container	6
Tomatoes, sauerkraut, canned	6
Other vegetables, canned (including dry beans and dry peas)	18
Cereals and baked goods:	
Ready-to-eat cereals:	
In metal container	12
In original paper package	1
Uncooked cereal (quick-cooking or instant):	
In metal container	24
In original paper package	12
Hydrogenated (or antioxidant-treated) fats, vegetable oil	12
Sugars, sweets, nuts:	
Sugar	will keep indefinitely
Hard candy, gum	18
Nuts, canned	12
Instant puddings	12
Miscellaneous:	
Coffee, tea, cocoa (instant)	18
Dry cream product (instant)	12
Bouillon products	12
Flavored beverage powders	24
Salt	will keep indefinitely
Flavoring extracts (e.g., pepper)	24
Soda, baking powder	12

SAMPLE MEAL PLANS: *No Cooking Facilities*

	First day	Second day	Third day
MORNING			
	Citrus fruit juice.[1]	Fruit juice.[1]	Grapefruit segments.[1]
	Ready-to-eat cereal.	Corned beef hash.[1]	Ready-to-eat cereal.
	Milk, cold coffee,[2] or tea.[2]	Crackers.	Vienna sausage.[1]
	Crackers.	Spread.	Milk, cold coffee,[2] or tea.[2]
	Peanut butter or other spread.	Milk, cold coffee,[2] or tea.[2]	
NOON			
	Spaghetti with meat sauce.[1]	Baked beans.[1]	Chile con carne with beans.[1]
	Green beans.[1]	Brown bread.[1]	Crackers.
	Crackers.	Tomatoes.[1]	Fruit.[1]
	Spread.	Fruit.[1]	Cookies.
	Milk, cold coffee,[2] or tea.[2]	Milk, cold coffee,[2] or tea.[2]	Milk, cold coffee,[2] or tea.[2]
BETWEEN MEALS			
	Fruit-flavored drink or fruit drink.	Milk.	Tomato juice.
NIGHT			
	Lunch meat.[1]	Pork and gravy.[1]	Sliced beef.[1]
	Sweetpotatoes.[1]	Corn.[1]	Macaroni and cheese.[1]
	Applesauce.[1]	Potatoes.[1]	Peas and carrots.[1]
	Milk, cold coffee,[2] or tea.[2]	Instant pudding.	Crackers.
	Candy.	Fruit juice.[1]	Milk, cold coffee,[2] or tea.[2]

[1] Canned.   [2] Instant.

SAMPLE MEAL PLANS: *Limited Cooking Facilities*

	First day	Second day	Third day
MORNING			
	Citrus fruit juice.[1] Ready-to-eat cereal. Milk. Hot coffee,[2] tea,[2] or cocoa.[2]	Citrus fruit juice.[1] Hot cereal (quick-cooking). Milk. Hot coffee,[2] tea,[2] or cocoa.[2]	Prunes.[1] Ready-to-eat cereal. Milk. Crackers. Cheese. Hot coffee,[2] tea,[2] or cocoa.[2]
NOON			
	Vegetable soup.[1] Potato salad.[1] Crackers. Ham spread.[1] Milk. Candy bar.	Beef-and-vegetable stew.[1] Green beans.[1] Crackers. Peanut butter. Milk.	Chile con carne with beans.[1] Tomatoes.[1] Crackers. Hot coffee,[2] tea,[2] or cocoa.[2]
BETWEEN MEALS			
	Fruit-flavored drink or fruit drink.	Tomato juice.[1]	Fruit-flavored drink or fruit drink.
NIGHT			
	Beef and gravy.[1] Noodles.[1] Peas and carrots.[1] Instant pudding. Hot coffee,[2] tea,[2] or cocoa.[2]	Tuna fish,[1] cream of celery soup,[1] mixed sweet pickles [1]—combined in one dish. Fruit.[1] Cookies. Hot coffee,[2] tea,[2] or cocoa.[2]	Lunch meat.[1] Hominy.[1] Applesauce.[1] Cookies. Peanuts. Hot coffee,[2] tea,[2] or cocoa.[2]

[1] Canned.   [2] Instant.

You may want to label cans and containers with the date of purchase and the approximate date when the particular item should be replaced by a new supply. Suggested charts for keeping a record of your family food reserves are given on pages 83 thru 90 of this book.

Equipment for Cooking and Serving

You need to have ready certain equipment for emergency cooking and serving.

A suggested list includes: a small, compact cooking unit, such as the ones used by campers; one or two cooking pans; disposable knives, forks, and spoons; paper plates, towels, cups and napkins; can and bottle openers; nursing bottles and nipples if there is a baby in the family; measuring cup; medicine dropper for measuring water purifier; matches; and a pocket knife.

If you already have plastic dishes, cups, forks, knives, and spoons, you may want to use them instead of disposable tableware. They would probably take less space to store, but water for washing them might not be available after an attack.

If disposable serving dishes and eating utensils are used, each family will need to estimate the number required for a 2 weeks' period.

Store your emergency cooking and serving equipment with your reserve food supply or near it.

WATER

You and your family can get along for quite a while without food, but only for a short time without water. Store a 2 weeks' supply of water for each member of your family NOW.

In moderate weather a person engaged in sedentary activity, consuming an average diet 15 percent of which is protein, requires a minimum of one-half gallon of water per day for drinking and food preparation, or 7 gallons for a 2 weeks' period. In contrast, half this amount of water is required in a survival diet.

Some of the need for liquids can be met by storing large quantities of fruit juice and soft drinks.

If you want to have water available for bathing, brushing teeth, and dishwashing, it should be of the same quality as water stored for drinking, and must be stored in addition to the amount mentioned above. Another 7 gallons of water is recommended for such purposes.

Some of your water requirements could be met by making use of the water in home hot-water tanks and toilet tanks.

At the time of attack, water in these tanks would be safe to use. Know the location of your main incoming water valve so you can shut it off if directed by local health authorities, to prevent the entrance of contaminated water. As a safety measure the valve on the gasline to your hot-water heater should be turned off also.

Water from a hot-water tank can be obtained by opening the drain cock at the bottom of the tank. To get a free flow of water with the water inlet valve turned off, you may need to vent the tank by turning on a faucet somewhere on the waterline. Some hot-water tanks are automatically vented.

Safe Sources of Water for Storage

It is of the utmost importance that water stored for emergency use be clean. Any water that has been tested and approved by health au-

thorities would be safe to store.

If there is any question about the safety or cleanliness of the water you intend to store or if it has not been tested and approved by health authorities, it must be purified before it is stored.

How to Purify Water

Boiling.—The safest method of purifying water is to boil it vigorously for 1 to 3 minutes to destroy bacteria that might be present. Boiling, however, does *not* destroy radioactivity. To improve the taste of the water after it has been boiled, pour the boiled water from one clean container to another several times.

Easy bleach method.—Any household bleach solution that contains hypochlorite, a chlorine compound, as its only active ingredient will purify water easily and inexpensively.

Bleach solutions with 5.25 percent of sodium hypochlorite are most common. They are available in grocery stores. Add the bleach solution to the water in any clean container in which it can be thoroughly mixed by stirring or shaking. The following table shows the proper amount of a 5.25-percent solution to add to water.

Amount of water	Amount of solution to add to—	
	Clear water	Cloudy water
1 quart (¼ gallon).	2 drops.	4 drops.
1 gallon_____	8 drops.	16 drops.
5 gallons_____	½ teaspoon.	1 teaspoon.

Add the chlorine solution to the water and stir, then let the mixture stand for 30 minutes. After this length of time the water should still have a distinct taste or smell of chlorine. If this taste or smell is not present, add another dose of the solution to the water and let the water stand another 15 minutes. The taste or smell of chlorine in water thus treated is a sign of safety. If you cannot detect chlorine in the water you are trying to purify by this method, do not store it. The chlorine solution may have weakened through age or for some other reason.

Iodine or tablet purification.—

If you have ordinary household 2-percent tincture of iodine in your home medicine chest, you can use it to purify small quantities of water. Add 3 drops of tincture of iodine to each quart of clear water, 6 drops to each quart of cloudy water. For a gallon, add 12 drops for clear water, 24 drops for cloudy water. Stir thoroughly.

Water-purification tablets that release chlorine or iodine can be used safely to purify water. They are inexpensive and can be bought at most sporting goods stores and some drugstores.

If you use water-purification tablets, follow the directions on the package. Usually 1 tablet is sufficient for 1 quart of water; double the dosage if the water is cloudy.

Storing Water Reserves

Store your water reserves in thoroughly washed, clean containers, preferably of heavy plastic with tight-fitting caps, or in glass jugs or bottles with screw tops. Metal containers tend to give water an unpleasant taste.

You may want to buy 5-gallon containers of rigid plastic or glass for water storage. The plastic containers have the advantage of being shatterproof and lighter in weight than glass jugs.

Pack glass containers tightly against damage or shock. Put newspapers, excelsior, or other packing material between the containers to keep them from coming in contact with one another.

Clean water stored in this way should remain palatable for an indefinite period. It is advisable to check the containers every few months for leaks. At the same time check the water for cloudiness or other undesirable appearance or undesirable taste. If undesirable appearances or tastes have developed, the water should be changed.

```
WARNING

   Water that has been con-
taminated by radioactive ma-
terial should not be used unless
no alternate supply is avail-
able. The danger from water
contaminated in this way is
greatest immediately a f t e r
fallout deposition. Infants
and children are more at risk
from such water than are
adults.
   Water from springs and
covered wells could be used.
```

OUR FAMILY FOOD RESERVE

Kind of food	Amount stored	Date purchased	Suggested replacement date

OUR FAMILY FOOD RESERVE

Kind of food	Amount stored	Date purchased	Suggested replacement date

OUR FAMILY FOOD RESERVE

Kind of food	Amount stored	Date purchased	Suggested replacement date

OUR FAMILY FOOD RESERVE

Kind of food	Amount stored	Date purchased	Suggested replacement date

OUR FAMILY FOOD RESERVE

Kind of food	Amount stored	Date purchased	Suggested replacement date

OUR FAMILY FOOD RESERVE

Kind of food	Amount stored	Date purchased	Suggested replace-ment date

OUR FAMILY FOOD RESERVE

Kind of food	Amount stored	Date purchased	Suggested replacement date

89

OUR FAMILY FOOD RESERVE

Kind of food	Amount stored	Date purchased	Suggested replacement date

STEP NUMBER FOUR

There is strength in unity. If you have trusted friends, discuss these matters with them. If they see things as you do, work out a program with them for mutual assistance and cooperation. Take Red Cross courses in first aid and Civil Defense courses in survival and emergency preparation. All major cities have such courses available and generally without charge. If you cannot take the courses, at least purchase a Red Cross First-Aid Manual and study it.

STEP NUMBER FIVE

Prepare to defend yourself, your life and your property, especially if you live in a large city. This may seem quite rash, but the time may very well come when you will think that it is the most sane suggestion anyone ever gave you. Our reaction to such thoughts are relative to our experiences. Comparatively few of us have ever had to fight to defend our life. Because of this, the thought of kill or be killed is shocking and repulsive. This is as it ought to be. Our nation would be in a sad state indeed if the idea of reverting back to the law of the jungle were not repulsive to most of its citizens. However, we are not talking about your reverting to the law of the jungle; we are talking about when others revert to that law and force you to. If you violate the law, they will kill you. You must face up to these facts. They will be the facts of life, or death.

Weapons are dangerous. They are dangerous to you as well as to your enemy. Find out where there is a gun club. Become familiar with the weapon you choose. The more familiar and experienced you become with your weapon, the less dangerous it will be to you and the more dangerous it will be to your enemy. Inasmuch as you will be a defender and not an aggressor, you will not need a large, powerful, long-range weapon. A small rapid-fire .22 calibre rifle will be your best bet. It is light weight enough that a woman or youth can learn to handle it easily. It does not have so much recoil that it would be damaging to a youth or woman, but a recoil pad could be added to the butt of the rifle stock to cushion any shock. The ammunition is small, light weight and inexpensive. A long rifle cartridge with hollow nose bullet will stop any aggressor. Large quantities of ammunition can be conveniently stored and carried. A weapon may become an absolute necessity in the securing of game animals for meat in times of severe deprivation. By all means, make sure that all who are to handle the weapon are thoroughly trained by an expert instructor. You can find a gun club near you that can help you by contacting the American Rifleman's Association. And of course, always make sure that the weapon is unloaded when not in use and stored where no child can possibly have access to it.

STEP NUMBER SIX

For those who live in large cities and metropolitan areas, it will be unsafe in times of a depression. You will have to be the judge of the area in which you live as to how suitable and safe it will be. In 1969 I moved to Utah from Los Angeles, California, because I no longer considered it safe in the light of what I knew was sure to come.

Unless your home at the present is in an unusually well-situated location, like a prime spot for the erection of a shopping center right away, there is little economical advantage to owning your own home, especially if the area might be unsafe in a serious national economic crisis. The increasing value of most homes is due to inflation and not due to genuine appreciation of value of the home itself. The same investment would probably return just as well in any other sound financial program. In addition to this, rising property taxes and insurance costs generally offset any gains normally made. Therefore there is, as a general rule, no financial advantage to owning your own home, particularly in an area that will prove unsafe.

It would be my suggestion that you sell your home and purchase a retreat home at least 200 miles from a large city such as Los Angeles, Dallas, or Chicago. It should not be completely isolated; that too would be unsafe. It need not be elaborate, but it should be comfortable and well-stocked with provisions. A small rural community where property values are not especially high would be your best bet. Occasional weekend vacations and holidays spent there will help you get accustomed to it. Improve it to suit yourself. An older home that you can fix up a little, a bare lot with a modern cabin, a mobil home--it's all up to you; but a place to go when times get rough might be the difference between heaven and hell on earth. Attending a local church on the weekends you are able to spend there might help you to build some friendships with some mighty fine people you will need in the future.

STEP NUMBER SEVEN

Once you have established a place to live through the trials of the depression, whether it is your present home or a retreat many miles away, *you will need to prepare yourself to live from one to two years without any outside income or vital necessities.* Again, a good safe water supply will be a necessity. You may want to put down a small well. In some areas, potable water can be reached 30 to 50 ft. below the surface of the ground. Specially pointed well heads and well pipes can be obtained from many sources, including Sears and Roebuck, which, with simple instructions, will enable you to drive the pipe into the ground and create a simple well for domestic purposes.

You will want to include a substantial supply of seeds for a vegetable garden. Growing your own food may be the only realistic way of providing for your needs. If you are not experienced in vegetable gardening, you may want to purchase a book that will serve as a guide. Inquiry from people in the area who have experience will yield many tips on the right time to plant, the kind of plants and varieties that do best in that area, and the best methods of cultivation and fertilization. Different areas and different soils have different requirements, so it will be well to do a little checking before you find out that you have a big supply of the wrong things. Remember, many people are not going to be as farsighted as you. They may not have or be able to get seeds or gardening utensils. They may want some of yours. A few extra in your supply might be very good bartering agents. Seeds that you bought for a quarter a year earlier could easily be worth five dollars in cash, commodities or labor. Seeds and food will be more valuable than actual money in many instances. Whatever you do, don't forget the garden forks, spades, rakes and hoes. The Indians got along without them, but they had a mighty tough time doing it too.

Foods that are grown in a garden are delicious, but they don't keep for very long. You will need a method of preserving them. There are three basic ways--freezing, canning and drying.

Because of the undependability of electrical power during the severe depression, it is best not to count on using any appreciable amount of frozen foods, because without power they will thaw and spoil rapidly.

Home canning is the best way of preserving foods at home. This will require both bottles and lids. The bottles and the retaining rings can be used over and over again, but the lids can only be used once, and so it will require a supply two to three times as great as the number of bottles you will have. Canning is rather specialized, and anyone contemplating it should either gain experience under the tutelage of an experienced hand or write to the Dept. of Agriculture, Washington D.C., and ask for their booklets on home canning. Booklets on vegetable and fruit gardening, poultry growing, and raising rabbits are also available.

One method of preserving food that is overlooked a lot these days is the oldest one, and that is the drying method. Since this requires the least amount of civilized equipment, it is the most dependable one in an emergency. An old refrigerator or a cabinet built to about that size will work just fine. Shelves that are really trays with one-quarter inch mesh screen wire for the bottoms are installed every 3 to 4 inches apart. They need to be removable. Fine screen wire covered vent holes on the top and bottom of the cabinet keep out flies and allow the air to circulate through the cabinet and dry the fruit and vegetables. Where gas or electric heat is available along with a fan, drying can be greatly facilitated. Under truly primitive circumstances, a fire in an outdoor fireplace beneath the drying cabinet will help, but do not allow the smoke to pass through the cabinet, just the heat.

Hard items such as peas, beans and carrots will need to be steamed first, then dried. Heavy skinned fruits and vegetables such as apples and turnips should be peeled. Soft fruits such as berries and peaches need no preparation except cutting. Meat can also be dried very effectively. It will keep almost indefinitely when properly cured. Any meat will do-- beef, deer, elk, rabbit, squirrel, chicken, turkey. Cut the meat into thin strips about one-half inch thick, cutting *across* the grain. Skew on a wire and place into a pot of already boiling brine water, made with one cup of salt to one gallon of water. Leave in the water for a few minutes until all of the red color is gone, remove and drain. Dry in the cabinet as with the fruits and vegetables. However, in this case, the smoke can pass through the dryer to flavor the meat. If the smoke is allowed to pass through the meat, do not use any of the trees which produce resin, such as pine and fir. Use apple, maple, willow, hickory, birch or any other such wood. Resin woods will cause the meat to become so bitter it cannot be eaten. Once dried hard, store it in glass or plastic containers and keep dry. Always keep insects away from meat while processing it.

All of the previous information with regard to the two-week emergency food storage plan is applicable to a longer-range one. However, in a long-range program you will want to add large quantities of wheat, flour, milk, beans, sugar, honey and peanut butter.

WHEAT

It should be grade no. 1 with a protein content of at least 11.5 percent and a moisture content 10 percent or lower; and it should be cleaned of foreign particles for human consumption. It should be stored in clean metal or plastic containers, 5 gallon size are the most convenient with lids that are airtight. Grain, as well as nuts, beans, peas, etc., can be heated in a shallow pan or tray three-quarters inch deep for 20 minutes at 150 degrees in an oven with the door slightly ajar. This will release excess moisture and kill potential insect eggs. Put dry ice in the bottom of the container; pour wheat, beans or peas in on top--the dry ice should be about the size of a 50 cent piece--leave the lid ajar for about 10 hours; then seal tightly. With a mixed diet of other foods, an adult will use 300 lbs. of wheat per year.

FLOUR

While wheat prepared as above will keep almost indefinitely, flour is not good for storage past about a year as it begins to go stale in flavor. Store in clean metal or plastic containers which seal airtight. Putting a bay leaf in the flour helps to maintain flavor and discourage insects. Wheat grinders are available through most health food stores, both power and hand, to convert wheat into fresh flour. Hand grinders are preferable, as the power source could fail. A year's supply is 100 lbs. of flour per adult.

MILK

Milk can be stored as canned milk and will last approximately one year. It should be turned every month or so. Powdered milk should be of the top grade with the lowest moisture content possible. Package in heavy plastic bags holding about 5 lbs. of powdered milk. As much air as possible should be removed and the bags heat-sealed. Such milk will store up to two years without the quality being affected. Vacuum-sealed cans will keep for a long period of time. These are commercially prepared. About 80 lbs. of powdered milk per person is the amount required for one year.

BEANS

In this category would fall all types of dried beans and peas. Soybeans are an excellent source of protein. A variety of beans can be stored as indicated with the wheat, and an aggregate total of 150 lbs. per person per year is sufficient.

SUGAR

Granulated white sugar stores better than brown. However, brown is much more nutritious. As with powdered milk, it should be heat-sealed in heavy plastic bags in 5 to 10 lb. quantities. Hardened sugar can be softened upon opening by putting a sliced apple in with the sugar and leaving it there. About 60 lbs. per person per year is needed.

HONEY

Honey is a good, nutritious sugar substitute. Five and 10 lb. cans are the most convenient. About 50 lbs. per person per year is sufficient. Pure crystalline honey that has no water added will keep indefinitely.

PEANUT BUTTER

This is high in protein and is a flavorful item which can be used in many ways. Combined with powdered milk, it makes a high-protein energy bar that tastes like candy. Peanut butter should be of top variety and should not be a spread with a high content of vegetable oil. Peanut butter should be turned every two months to prevent settling. About 50 lbs. per person per year is adequate.

CANNED GOODS

Canned goods for a family of five will average per day, 2 soup, 2 vegetable, 1 meat, and 2 fruit. Shortening for a year will consist of 12 - 3 lb. cans for a family of five. Juices will average 5 cans per week. Also needed are 6 cans of baking powder, 4 gallons of clorox for water sterilization. These will serve as a good guide in preparing your year's supply of food.

MISC. ITEMS

In addition to food you will need alcohol, ammonia, antiseptic solution, aspirin, bandaids, bandages, bowl cleaner, cotton, ear drops, epson salts, lysol, paragoric, safety pins, sanitary napkins, shampoo, thermometers, toothbrushes, toothpaste, tweezers, water purification tablets, specific medications and miscellaneous health aids.

You will also need an ax, basic hand tools, emergency cook stove and fuel, emergency light and fuel and mantles, emergency heater, fishing equipment, flashlight and extra batteries, light bulbs, paper plates and cups, pens and paper, portable radio, rifle and shells, sewing supplies, shoe laces, and wheat grinder.

You will also need an extra supply of blankets, boots, coats, dresses, pillow cases, sheets, shirts, shoes, stockings, trousers, towels and undergarments.

The preceding information is not given as though it were a complete guide, but it should serve as a warning as to the magnitude of the job it will be to try to supply the needs of a family over a long period of time when the normal channels of supply are interrupted or destroyed for days, weeks or months. Since the possibility of such a thing occurring in the very near future is very real, it will behoove you to make a serious effort to compile a complete list of those items you will need first and begin to set them aside just as soon as possible. Remember, it is better to be ready years too soon than to be one day too late.

COMMERCIAL STORAGE FOODS

For those who wish to avoid the difficulty involved in selecting the right foods and making sure they are properly packaged and rotated so they won't spoil, you will want to look into one of the several food storage programs that are available. Several companies are now producing specially processed foods with the right amount of moisture. They are packaged to give them an almost indefinite no-spoil shelf-life. These products are then reconstituted with water to give them a surprisingly pleasant and agreeable taste and consistency.

These food programs have several distinct advantages: 1. Because so much of the moisture is removed; they are concentrated and thus the bulk is greatly reduced. For those with limited storage space, this is an important factor. 2. Also because of the moisture removal, they are lighter in weight, making it easy for a woman or child to move the food supply in an emergency. 3. They are generally packaged in nutritionally balanced food programs. 4. They also generally have a variety of foods and flavors to insure an appealing diet. 5. They are properly packaged so that spoilage is at an absolute minimum. 6. They are a ''store 'em and forget 'em till you need 'em'' type of an item.

The primary disadvantages are the slight increase in cost to pay for the extra processing and packaging, and the need for a good supply of water. While these foods can easily be eaten without being reconstituted with water, there is a need, when water is very difficult to obtain, for the moisture derived from regularly canned foods. If you are where getting a gallon of water a day per person is no problem, these foods would be ideal.

Certainly these foods have a place in any storage program; the degree will have to be determined by each individual. You should be able to find a local outlet for such foods.

STEP NUMBER EIGHT

Do not keep money in a savings account in either a savings and loan or bank. Leave only enough money in your checking account to pay your bills each month and that is all. When the panic strikes, no bank will be safe. Do not maintain a safety deposit box in a banking type of an institution. All of your assets may be frozen or confiscated by executive action of the President or absconded with by a bank associate or a mob. It has happened many times before, right here in the United States, and it is about to happen again. There are not enough reserves either in the bank, the Federal Reserve, or the FDIC to begin to cover all of the withdrawals if a panic should occur. *Maintain only enough paper currency to meet your immediate needs.*

STEP NUMBER NINE

Convert your paper currency into a ready reserve of from $250 to $1,000 in silver coins. These coins will cost you a premium, that is, more than their face value; but you can hardly expect someone who has a silver dime to give it to you for one of the copper tokens they now call a dime that is only worth a fraction of what the silver one is.

There are three kinds or categories of silver coins: first is Numismatic Silver coins, coins that are rare and carry a very inflated price because of their rarity. This is a poor investment because their value will drop heavily during a depression. The second is Silver Commodity coins, coins that are being held in reserve for the expected profit that can be taken when the price of silver bullion rises high enough to warrant selling them to the bullion market to be melted down. The third type is the Junk Silver coin. These coins are sold, generally in $1,000 quantities. They are silver coins that have been gleaned from all of the coins in circulation and have no special value above and beyond their silver content. You can purchase these coins at the lowest price for your purpose of having ready cash in silver. They will have great value when the depression hits and no one will accept the paper currency or the nickel-clad copper tokens. Then these coins will have a recognizable value. These coins may be purchased through a local coin dealer or a coin exchange. Local coin shops will charge more but will sell smaller quantities of coins. Coin exchanges will generally give terms on quantity purchases, holding the coins until you have completed payment. Current market prices for silver coins can usually be obtained from the want-ad section of the Sunday edition of Los Angeles and New York newspapers under ''coin dealers.''

It will be important that as few people as possible know that you are buying silver coins. Your coins will probably be safer under your own control than under someone elses. Do not put all your eggs in one basket--several caches, hiding places, are better than one. Make sure that more than one person in the family knows where the coins are. That way, if an accident or death should occur to one member of the family, it will not render the coins inaccessible. A hidden floor safe buried in concrete--install it yourself--is probably the best place for your valuables.

STEP NUMBER TEN

For those who have large sums of wealth in stocks, bonds, property, savings accounts and other assets that will greatly devalue, a serious problem arises as to the safest place to put such wealth if it were to be liquidated now while a decent return could be expected. The author feels that silver bullion offers the most secure investment possible in these turbulent times.

Great effort is now being made in the popular media to make it appear that silver is not a good investment. Do not be deceived. It is true that some speculative purchasing may temporarily push the price up out of proportion; any sudden and sharp rise in the price is bound to be inflationary and have to readjust itself. However, the basic value of silver always has continued and always will continue to rise. Silver is increasing in value, not because of its use as money--after all, it has been more than five years since the United States has been minting silver coins--it is rising in value because the world keeps finding more uses for silver than the mining industry can supply. Silver is one of the most useful metals in existence; that is why it is valuable.

Remember that in the '29 crash, the financial genius, Bernard Baruch, financial consultant to numerous Presidents, emerged a multi-billionaire because he had almost all of his money in silver--almost one-fifth of the world's visible silver at that time.[28] Those who saw him buying that silver in '28, the year before the Crash, thought he was crazy for not staying in the market that seemed to be doing so well and making a killing on stocks and bonds. Of course, when the dust had settled from the Crash and the price of silver doubled, he emerged, not as crazy, but as a genius.

I advocate the ownership of silver, not merely as an investment, but also as a protection against the loss of your life's earnings and savings. When paper currency greatly or even completely loses its value, you will need something that still has value to use as money. Silver will not only have retained its value but will actually have gone up in value, relative to the depreciating value of other forms of wealth.

In writing about the terrible consequences of unbacked inflationary currency, John Maynard Keynes, the father of the economic theories that got us into this mess, wrote:

A sentiment of trust in the legal money of the State is so deeply implanted in the citizens of all countries that they cannot but believe that someday this money must recover a part at least of its former value. To their minds it appears that value is inherent in money as such, and they do not comprehend that the real wealth, which this money might have stood for, has been dissipated once and for all. This sentiment is supported by the various legal regulations with which the governments endeavor to control internal prices, and so to preserve some purchasing power for their legal tender. Thus the force of law preserves a measure of immediate purchasing power over some commodities and the force of sentiment maintains a willingness to hoard paper which is really worthless....If however, a government refrains from regulation and allows matters to take their course, essential commodities soon attain a level of price out of the reach of all but the rich, the worthlessness of the money becomes apparent, and the fraud upon the public can be concealed no longer. [29]

It is apparent from reading those lines penned by Mr. Keynes that he was talking about the very financial conditions our nation is experiencing at the present time. Soon the "worthlessness of the money becomes apparent, and the fraud upon the public can be concealed no longer." It is my sincere hope that you will be able to see what is happening and not, as he says, show a "willingness to hoard paper which is really worthless." Do not be deceived. Silver is your best money protection in the coming crash.

In spite of the solid and reputable appearance of Swiss banks, the author has some strong reservations about dealing with these international bankers and the degree of safety your silver would have if stored in their vaults during a world financial crisis. In response to this concern, there are firms who recognize the need for storing silver here in the United States as a means of providing protection for those with large sums of cash. These firms will sell you pure silver ingots and have it stored for you in a bonded and certified vault. They will also sell your silver at the prevailing market price any time you want to sell, or you can take possession of as much or as little of it as you want any time you want. For those who want their silver in smaller units of value, there are handsome, troy ounce silver pieces that have been privately minted and silver bars as small as one ounce. If you wish assistance in contacting these firms, write to the Author at Wake-Up Publishing, P.O. Box 150, Provo, Utah 84601.

INVESTMENTS TO STAY AWAY FROM

LIFE INSURANCE AND RETIREMENT

Stay in the 5-year-term bracket.

MORTGAGES

Foreclosures are high in a depression. But what is the value to you to loan on a $20,000 house only to foreclose on one that has devalued to $10,000? How many years will it take to get your money back, let alone show a profit? The same can be said for owning commercial property. It's great in inflation, but with a depression it's bad news. Businesses are failing; they can't pay their rent; stores and offices are vacant all over town; violence and damage destroy whatever value there was in the property. The fancier and more luxurious the property, the sooner it will probably be vacated.

U.S. GOVERNMENT BONDS

Avoid them like the plague. The government is already broke, putting your hard-earned dollars in would be like throwing gasoline on the fire.

ART-JEWELRY AND DIAMONDS

Bad news, all luxury items go up in inflation and come way down during the depression.

LAND

With the exception of a reasonable amount of well-located agricultural land, you don't want to own a lot of property before a depression of the magnitude this one is going to be. It will devalue terribly, and it will be subject to vandalism. Buy all you want with silver for practically nothing in a depression.

COMMODITIES

Farm and metals, sold as a rule as futures, they aren't even good when the economy is good.

STOCKS-BONDS AND MUTUAL FUNDS

A real loser, the bottom is going to drop straight out, and many of these companies won't even be around, let alone show a profit.

By resisting the temptation to make that last buck on that last good deal, you may lose one or two marbles by leaving the game early. But if you leave the game one day too late, you may lose them all.

TWO THINGS YOU SHOULD DO

Now that you have read this book, there are two things you should do.

1. WARN OTHERS

The first thing is to warn your family and friends to get ready for the coming crash and the terrible depression that will follow. Share the message of this book but do not attempt to force them to accept it. To do so will not help them and will only create feelings of bitterness. "A man convinced against his will is of the same opinion still," the old saying goes--and it is still true. You must recognize that there are always a great many people who refuse to be warned, refuse to heed danger signs and refuse to prepare for any coming emergency.

2. DO NOT PANIC

The second thing is to get ready, but do not panic. Follow the 10-step plan, step-by-step. Do what you can as fast as you can, but do not worry about that which remains undone. No matter what happens, if you have followed these steps carefully, you will know that you did the best you could with the means and time available to you. No one could ask or expect more from you.

There are people who read this book that will probably feel--and rightly so--that they should move to a different part of the country, that they should quit their job and sell their home. Others will want to liquidate investment and commercial holdings. Many people are in precarious positions and should do these things; but they should be done in a calm, well thought-out program. Do not quit a job without having a knowledge of where or how you can get another. "Look before you leap" is still good advice. Don't sell off investments and property in panic; make sure you are going to get a fair price; don't take just anything to get out.

DO NOT BE DECEIVED

During the months before the '72 elections, great effort will be made to make it appear that the economy has never been better. That is also the way it appeared just before the '29 crash. Do not be deceived; it is not real and it cannot last. Since the first edition of this book was published, there has already been a token devaluation of the American dollar. And that is exactly what it was--a token devaluation. Although it was labeled an 8 percent devaluation, the actual purchasing power of the American dollar overseas has declined an average of 10 percent.[30] This means it will cost you 10 percent more to purchase foreign goods and services. This small devaluation is only to condition the mind of the public that devaluation isn't so bad. To ease the pain of the increased cost of imports, the government removed the excise tax on imports. Of course this ruse can only be used once. It does not solve, but only compounds the problem. The loss of revenue from the excise tax and the election year tax cuts only increases the deficit spending of the government. Thus our financial problems continue to worsen.

DEVALUATION ADMITS
GOLD IS THE STANDARD

By devaluation, we have admitted that gold is still the world's standard of wealth. The pressure will continue to mount for more and more devaluation, until the value of the dollar--its purchasing power--is more in line with the amount of gold behind it.

Rep. Henry S. Reuss, a ranking member of the powerful House Banking Committee, stated four years ago, the U.S. "is never going to increase the price of gold," and thus devalue the dollar; but in a recent House speech, he declared that the U.S. must accept devaluation "as part of an appropriate solution to current international economic problems of the United States."[31] This changing view is reflected throughout the Congress by the easy vote by which devaluation has been accomplished. This is simply political double talk that means we as a nation are so broke that we must continue to accept less and less for the dollar. The American dollar is a paper tiger.

1971—LARGEST PAYMENTS DEFICIT

The greatest balance of payments deficit in the history of our nation was accumulated in 1971. This means that we spent 1.8 billion dollars more in foreign countries than they spent with us.[32] This means a flow of wealth going out of the country rather than in. This just adds that many billion dollars more to our international debt and gives the foreign nations a bigger club to hold over our head. The foreign nations must either buy American products with those dollars or hold them since they cannot redeem them for gold. Since Europe has been in a business recession for the past year with the growth rate of their gross national product dropping for the third year in a row and their stock markets ending up with an annual loss of as much as 22 percent in 1971, it is obvious that they must sell products, not buy them.[33] To spend dollars in America would increase their recession, and they aren't about to contribute to their own economic problems. Europe is in serious trouble economically and the United States is at her mercy.

BUDGET DEFICIT INCREASES

The fiscal year of 1971 ended with a whopping peacetime deficit of 23 billion dollars.[34] It was first estimated that the 1972 deficit would run in the neighborhood of 11.6 billion; now the revised estimate is 38.8 billion dollars.[35] The estimate for the 1973 budget is a plan to spend 25.5 billion dollars in deficit of income.[36] This will bring the four-year Nixon total to at least 90 billion dollars and more likely in excess of 100 billion dollars in debt.[37] This is more than *twice* the amount of debt incurred by this nation from its founding in 1776 through 1940, a period of 164 years. The ceiling on the National Debt was just raised another 20 billion by Congress, and Secretary Connally of the Treasury says he will be back next year asking for another increase. Obviously, there is no intention of running a financially sound government. With such an approach the day of reckoning just keeps moving up, closer and closer. There is no hope of averting the crash; it looks worse than ever.

G.N.P. VERSUS NATIONAL DEBT

Many economists attempt to cover up the problem of the rising national debt by stating that this is offset by the rising gross national product. However, this is a trick. It is like comparing apples and bananas. The combined wealth of the nation, both public and private, as reflected in the Gross National Product has risen a spectacular 300 percent in the last 20 years; however, even more spectacular has been the rise of the Net Public and Private Debt, which has risen 400 percent in the last 20 years.[38] This means that we as a nation are going into debt at a rate that is 25 percent in excess of our productive capacity. No matter where we turn, the answer is the same--the nation is going broke at an ever-increasing rate.

The President seeks to avoid the inevitable by playing a game of charades with the national budget, attempting to be a magician and pull wealth out of an empty hat. More than 5,000 years of human experience tell us that it cannot be done. Wealth must be created out of something of value; only nothing can be made from nothing.

ELECTION YEAR ANTICS

Just as I predicted on page 36, the money men are trying to pump up the economy with easier credit and more printing-press money. On February 9, 1972, before the Joint Congressional Economic Committee, Arthur Burns, chairman of the Federal Reserve Board, stated in prepared testimony: ''The Federal Reserve does not intend to let the present recovery falter for want of money or credit.''[39] The fact that the Federal Reserve has lowered their discount rate three times in four months in an unprecedented move to stimulate the economy is evidence that the Federal Reserve does indeed intend to pour in all the money they feel is necessary to stimulate the economy in an effort to make things look good.

As I pointed out on earlier pages, it is a very thin line between doing too much and not doing enough when the money people start manipulating the economy. In the above-mentioned hearing, Mr. Burns admitted that what he was doing was risky business. ''An unduly expanded monetary policy would be most unfortunate, particularly in view of the large federal budgetary deficits now projected,'' he stated. But as syndicated newspaper columnist Joseph R. Selvin points out in his column,

There are risks to the Federal Reserve's new gung-
ho drive to boost the money supply. The great danger is
that the Central Bank will go too far....Burns and his
colleagues have decided to gamble on doing too much
rather than too little. The threat of renewed inflation is a
problem for the future, but six percent unemployment
and the insistent prodding of a nervous, election-focused
White House are here and now.[40]

In a copyrighted article from the Washington Star, we find this interesting comment with regards to Mr. Burns' Congressional testimony: ''The legally independent Federal Reserve is under pressure from the Nixon administration to expand money and credit more rapidly.''[41]

Thus a massive election-year drive is on to inflate artificially the economy in order to make the Administration look good. But the cure will be worse than the disease, look out crash, here we come!

MANIPULATORS KNOW THE GAME

The man most responsible for the financial mess the United States is now in is John Maynard Keynes, creator of Keynesian economics. The question is, is the mess by design or by accident?

In the year 1920, Mr. Keynes published his first important work, *The Economic Consequences of the Peace.*[42] Most economists agree that this work is along the ''classic'' lines of economics--that is, dollar for dollar, pound for pound, balanced budgets and the gold standard, as a basis for a sound economy. Little is heard of this early work of Keynes today. Most disciples of Keynesian economics would probably like to bury it.

During the next decade Mr. Keynes was doing a lot of thinking and changing. By 1930, when he published his

112

Theory of Money, he had reversed his field. He had by this time gathered many disciples; not the least of them was Stuart Chase, author of a book in 1931, championing these new ideas in economics. The book Mr. Chase wrote was *A New Deal,* in which he stated among other interesting things, that the government would control the economy and that "the sixteen methods of becoming wealthy would be proscribed (punished)--by firing squad if necessary."[43] It was this same book from which Mr. Roosevelt took the name of his administration, the "New Deal." It was this same Mr. Chase who joined that administration, as a member of the National Resources Commission, and is credited with authoring the law that banned American citizens from owning gold coins.[44] But back to Mr. Keynes.

In 1936, Mr. Keynes published his most important work, *The General Theory of Employment, Interest and Money.*[45] Just before publishing his book, Keynes wrote to his friend George Bernard Shaw, the great Fabian Socialist and admirer of Stalin and Lenin, and said, "To understand my state of mind, however, you have to know that I believe myself to be writing a book on economic theory which will largely revolutionize--not I suppose at once, but in the course of the next ten years--the way the world thinks about economic problems."[46] Mr. Keynes, whose earlier works had been praised by Lenin, felt that he was writing a book that would "revolutionize" the world's thinking on economics.

The basis of the "General Theory" is that the government can print inflationary money at a very low cost and then place it into circulation through deficit spending and loans from the central banks. By regulating the interest rate, it can control the amount of money flowing into the economy, thereby regulating the employment rate. Now, in order to really understand how this concept was going to "revolutionize" the world, we must refer back to something that Keynes wrote in 1920:

> *Lenin is said to have declared that the best way to destroy the Capitalist System was to debauch the currency. By a continuing process of inflation, governments can confiscate, secretly and unobserved, an important part of the wealth of their citizens....Lenin was certainly right. There is no subtler, no surer means of overturning the existing basis of society than to debauch the currency. The process engages all the hidden forces of economic law on the side of destruction and does it in a manner which not one man in a million is able to diagnose.*[47]

Thus the man who created the modern concept of the government's deliberately printing inflationary money and going into debt under the guise of increasing employment and prosperity knew all along, and even admitted it in writing, that the theory "engages all the hidden forces of economic law on the side of destruction," that those in control of that process of inflation--in our case, the Federal Reserve--could "confiscate, secretly and unobserved, an important part of the wealth of their citizens"; that "there is no subtler, nor surer means of overturning the existing basis of society than to debauch the currency"; and on top of that, that it "does it in a manner which not one man in a million is able to diagnose."

Keynes' entire "General Theory" is nothing more than a carefully disguised plan to break down the Capitalist System. For he also stated,

> *...we are thus faced in Europe with the spectacle of an* extraordinary weakness *on the part of the great capitalist class, which has emerged from the industrial triumphs of the nineteenth century, and seemed a very few years ago* our all-powerful master....*Perhaps it is historically true*

that no order of society ever perishes save by its own hand. In the complexer world of Western Europe the Imminent Will may achieve its ends more subtly and bring in the revolution no less inevitably through a Klotz or a George than by the Intellectualisms, too ruthless and self-conscious for us, of the bloodthirsty philosophers of Russia.[48]

How plainly Keynes reveals his true feelings, referring to the "capitalist class" as "our all-powerful master" who will perish at the hands of a Judas, one who would rise up "more subtly and bring in the revolution no less inevitably" than the "bloodthirsty philosophers of Russia." It is interesting that Keynes sought to fulfill his own prophecy of a society perishing by its own hand, as he came forward as a capitalist economist, only to advance an economic program that he knew would bring about the financial destruction of the capitalist nations that embrace it.

The greatest tragedy is that President Nixon has thoroughly embraced Keynesian economics as the official economic policy of his Administration. He is leading this nation down the path of economic suicide. The death knell will sound sometime after the 1972 elections, most likely sometime between mid-1973 and mid-1974.

It is intended that the enormous problems that will result will be used as a leverage to bring about greater controls and a world socialist government. But once the great depression starts; once the pent-up volcano of fear, suspicion and hate is unleashed, there will be no controlling it; like a fire out of control, it will rage across the face of this once great and proud nation.

WHAT CAN BE DONE

Many people wonder what can be done to prevent this tragedy. Nothing, absolutely nothing. The inflationary

115

money is already being poured into the economy by the millions of dollars, and the devastating results of that action will be an excruciating experience that will tear and strain at every fiber in the fabric of the nation.

While nothing can be done to prevent it, there are three things that can be done to minimize the harm that will be done.

1. Follow the ten-step program already outlined in this book so that you and your family will be prepared to live through the terrible readjustment period.

2. Spread the word to as many people as you can so that the greatest possible number can prepare for what lies ahead.

3. Work hard for the election of good, sensible, loyal, conservative Americans to city, state and especially national offices in the days ahead.

When in the course of human events, power hungry men sought to usurp the God given, inalienable rights of our forefathers, they rose to the occasion and gave to the world a Declaration of Independence. A declaration of the people, stating that "...when a long Train of Abuses and Usurpations, pursuing invariably the same Object, envinces a Design to reduce them under absolute Despotism, it is their Right, it is their Duty, to throw off such Governments, and to provide new Guard for their future security." Once again, we the people of America face the situation of power hungry men through a long Train of Abuses and Usurpations, pursuing the same Object, with a design to reduce us to a state of absolute Despotism, and rob us of all our God given inalienable rights. It is not only our Right but it is our Duty, not only to ourselves, but to our unborn generations that lie ahead to be prepared to rise up at the right moment and throw off all the Usurpations that have been attached to our Divinely inspired Constitution, and which like leeches are sapping the life and strength of our nation.

Soon a terrible economic calamity will befall this nation. A calamity that has been prepared for years as a means to reduce the once proud and free American people to the position of a starving Essau begging for food. Then will be introduced the ''new constitution'' which will offer us guaranteed food in exchange for a controlled society where ''crashes'' never occur. Unless we are prepared, we, like Essau, will exchange our Birthright of Freedom for a mess of pottage. With a 15 million dollar grant from the Ford Foundation, the ''new constitution'' has already been written. (For complete details see our book, *The Plot to Replace the Constitution).* Everything is in readiness and moving according to schedule. The plan is to give us a ''new constitution'' to celebrate the 200th anniversary of the birth of our nation in 1976. (The April 23, 1973 edition of *Newsweek* Magazine on page 13 has an article by a former Nixon Aide calling for just such a move.)

If you do not want to exchange your Birthright of Freedom for a mess of pottage in the form of a terrible new constitution, we respectfully suggest that you contact *Liberty Lobby, 300 Independence Ave. S.E., Washington, D.C. 20003.* When the economic collapse occurs, only those who have prepared for it will be ready to step into the vacuum of leadership that will be created. Only those with food, land to grow it, gold or silver with which to buy it, and are organized to provide responsible political leadership, only they will be able to lead the people of this nation away from the temptation to sell their Birthright of Freedom and go into bondage. Although we cannot stop the crash, if enough people become aware and work together, (both in and out of government); those who seek to use the coming disaster to gain control of the nation and emerge as the rulers of the world can be denied at least their final victory.

If the American people ever allow private banks to control the issue of currency, first by inflation, then by deflation, the banks and corporations that will grow up around them will deprive the people of all property until their children will wake up homeless on the continent their fathers conquered.[49]

— Thomas Jefferson

Remember that it is better to be ready years too soon than to be one day late. The life you save may be your own!

ORDER BLANK FOR THIS AND OTHER BOOKS BY ROBERT L. PRESTON ON LAST PAGE.

HOW TO PREPARE
FOR THE COMING CRASH
—BIBLIOGRAPHY—

1. Cleon Skousen, *The Naked Capitalist*, p. 10.
2. Carroll Quigley, *Tragedy and Hope*, pp. 71-72.
3. Cleon Skousen, *Op Cit.*, pp. 24-25.
4. Wickliffe Vennard, *The Federal Reserve Hoax*, pp. 96-97.
5. Lansbury, *My Life*, Quote: Keynes at Harvard, p. 22.
6. Arsene de Goulevitch, *Czarism and the Revolution.*
7. Jacob Schiff, *New York Journal-American*, February 3, 1949.
8. Cleon Skousen, *Op Cit.*, p. 41.
9. B.C. Forbes, *Men Who Are Making America*, p. 401.
   Stephen Birmingham, *Our Crown*, p. 415.
10. Cleon Skousen, *Op Cit.*, p. 17.
11. Frank Vanderlip, *Saturday Evening Post*, February 9, 1935, p. 25.
12. Jules Akels, *The Rockefeller Billions*, p. 285.
13. Charles A. Lindbergh, Sr., *Congressional Record*, December 22, 1913.
    Henry Cabot Lodge, Sr., *Congressional Record*, June 10, 1932.
14. Marriner S. Eccles, "House Banking and Currency Committee Report," June 17 and 19, 1942, pp. 25-26.
    H.S. Kenan, *The Federal Reserve Bank*, pp. 48-58.
15. "A Primer on Money," *House Document* 72-504, pp. 4-5.
16. Congressional Report entitled: "State of the Economy and Policies for Full Employment," p. 524.
17. *U.S. News & World Report*, May 5, 1969.
18. Harry Browne, *How To Profit from the Coming Devaluation.*
19. Congressman Louis T. McFadden, *Congressional Record*, June 15, 1933.
20. Ferdinand Lunberg, *America's 60 Families.*
21. Murray Rothbard, *Economic Depressions: Causes and Cures.*

22. William Bryan, *The United States' Unresolved Monetary and Political Problems.*
23. Carroll Quigley, *Op Cit.,* p. 72.
24. Cleon Skousen, *The Naked Communist.*
25. Skousen, *Ibid.*
26. Harry Browne, *How to Profit from the Coming Devaluation.*
27. John T. Flynn, *Men of Wealth.*
28. Curtis B. Dall, *F.D.R. My Exploited Father-In-Law,* pp. 73-74.
29. John Maynard Keynes, *The Economic Consequences of the Peace,* pp. 239-240.
30. "Money Pact," *U.S. News & World Report,* p. 12.
31. "Devaluation: Once Taboo, Now 'In' Thing," *Deseret News,* January 13, 1972, p. 8A.
32. "Money Pact," *Op Cit.,* p. 13.
33. "Signs of Recession in Europe," *U.S. News & World Report,* November 29, 1971, pp. 30-31.
34. "Nixon Budget--Another Deficit," *U.S. News & World Report,* January 17, 1972, p. 40.
35. "Nixon Budget, More Spending, More Red Ink," *U.S. News & World Report,* January 31, 1972, p. 27.
36. *Ibid.*
37. U.S. Treasury Department Figures, See any Almanac or Year Book.
38. U.S. Department of Commerce, See any Almanac or Year Book.
39. "Federal Reserve Chief Vows, 'Enough Credit,'" *Deseret News,* February 10, 1972.
40. Joseph R. Selvin, *Deseret News,* January 11, 1972, p. 14A.
41. "Federal Reserve Chief Vows, 'Enough Credit,'" *Op Cit.*
42. John Maynard Keynes, *The Economic Consequences of the Peace,* 1920.
43. Stuart Chase, *A New Deal,* p. 163.
44. John A. Stormer, *None Dare Call It Treason,* p. 186.
45. John Maynard Keynes, *The General Theory of Employment, Interest and Money,* 1936.
46. Harrod, *Life of John Maynard Keynes,* p. 462.

47. John Maynard Keynes, *Economic Consequences of the Peace*, pp. 235-236.
48. *Ibid.*, pp. 237-238.
49. Thomas Jefferson, *The Writings of Thomas Jefferson*, Memorial Edition.

TWO MORE BOOKS

by

ROBERT L. PRESTON

**THE PLOT TO REPLACE
THE CONSTITUTION** 2.00
Robert L. Preston - A shocking expose of the
diabolical plot to instigate a national crisis
forcing Americans to give up their Birthright of
Freedom for a mess of pottage. 120 pp.

WAKE-UP AMERICA 2.00
Robert L. Preston - A carefully documented
expose of a power play by the super rich to rule
the United States in the near future through the
use of Communism. 120 pp.

ORDER BLANK

HAWKES PUBLICATIONS
156 W. 2170 S., Salt Lake City, Utah 84115

SHIP TO: _____

_____

_____

Books by Cleon Skousen:
____ . Naked Capitalist   2.00
____ . Naked Communist   3.50

Books by John D. Hawkes:
____ . New Testament Digest   2.00
____ . Art of Achieving Success   2.50
____ . Keys to Successful Dating

    10.00

Books by Richard L. Evans:
____ . Richard Evans' Quote Book   4.95
____ . Richard Evans' Quote Book -
    Gift Boxed   5.95
____ . Thoughts for 100 Days - Vol. I   3.50
____ . Thoughts for 100 Days - Vol. II   3.50
____ . Thoughts for 100 Days - Vol. III   3.50
____ . Thoughts for 100 Days - Vol. IV   3.50

Books by Helen Andelin:
____ . Fascinating Womanhood   5.95
____ . Fascinating Girl   6.95

Books by Other Authors:
____ . Beginnings (poetry)
    by Carol Lynn Pearson   2.95
____ . Handy Book for Genealogists
    by George Everton (hard)   5.80
____ . Harmon Killebrew--Baseball's
    Superstar   by Wayne Anderson   6.95
____ . He Walked the America's
    by L. Taylor Hansen   6.95
____ . Make a Treat with Wheat
    by Hazel Richards   1.95
____ . None Dare Call It Conspiracy
    by Gary Allen   1.00
____ . Readings for the Young at Heart
    by Laura M. Hawkes   2.95
____ . Rock 'n' Reality
    by E. Lynn Balmforth   2.50

ORDER BLANK FOR ROBERT L. PRESTON BOOKS ON BACK OF THIS PAGE.

ORDER BLANK FOR ROBERT L. PRESTON BOOKS

NAME _____

ADDRESS _____

CITY _____ STATE _____ ZIP _____

TITLE	QUANTITY	PRICE	AMOUNT
HOW TO PREPARE FOR THE COMING CRASH	___X___	___	___
BUILDING YOUR FORTUNE WITH SILVER	___X___	___	___
WAKE-UP AMERICA—IT'S LATER THAN YOU THINK	___X___	___	___
THE PLOT TO REPLACE THE CONSTITUTION	___X___	___	___

Postage .25

Total _____

1 thru 9 copies	2.00 each
10 thru 24 copies	1.80 "
25 thru 49 copies	1.70 "
60 thru 99 copies	1.60 "
100 copies	1.50 "

(Titles may be mixed for discounts; however, discounts are allowed only on single orders shipped to a single address. Orders to Canada must add 25 cents per book.)

ORDER SEVERAL
* * * * * * * * * *
Give to Friends and
Relatives — HELP
WAKE UP AMERICA

Make checks payable and send your order to:
Wake-Up Publishing Co., P.O. Box 150, Provo, Utah 84601